C-260   CAREER EXAMINATION SERIES

This is your
PASSBOOK for...

Food Service Worker

Test Preparation Study Guide
Questions & Answers

NATIONAL LEARNING CORPORATION®

COPYRIGHT NOTICE

This book is SOLELY intended for, is sold ONLY to, and its use is RESTRICTED to individual, bona fide applicants or candidates who qualify by virtue of having seriously filed applications for appropriate license, certificate, professional and/or promotional advancement, higher school matriculation, scholarship, or other legitimate requirements of education and/or governmental authorities.

This book is NOT intended for use, class instruction, tutoring, training, duplication, copying, reprinting, excerption, or adaptation, etc., by:

1) Other publishers
2) Proprietors and/or Instructors of "Coaching" and/or Preparatory Courses
3) Personnel and/or Training Divisions of commercial, industrial, and governmental organizations
4) Schools, colleges, or universities and/or their departments and staffs, including teachers and other personnel
5) Testing Agencies or Bureaus
6) Study groups which seek by the purchase of a single volume to copy and/or duplicate and/or adapt this material for use by the group as a whole without having purchased individual volumes for each of the members of the group
7) Et al.

Such persons would be in violation of appropriate Federal and State statutes.

PROVISION OF LICENSING AGREEMENTS – Recognized educational, commercial, industrial, and governmental institutions and organizations, and others legitimately engaged in educational pursuits, including training, testing, and measurement activities, may address request for a licensing agreement to the copyright owners, who will determine whether, and under what conditions, including fees and charges, the materials in this book may be used them. In other words, a licensing facility exists for the legitimate use of the material in this book on other than an individual basis. However, it is asseverated and affirmed here that the material in this book CANNOT be used without the receipt of the express permission of such a licensing agreement from the Publishers. Inquiries re licensing should be addressed to the company, attention rights and permissions department.

All rights reserved, including the right of reproduction in whole or in part, in any form or by any means, electronic or mechanical, including photocopying, recording, or by any information storage and retrieval system, without permission in writing from the Publisher.

Copyright © 2024 by
National Learning Corporation

212 Michael Drive, Syosset, NY 11791
(516) 921-8888 • www.passbooks.com
E-mail: info@passbooks.com

PUBLISHED IN THE UNITED STATES OF AMERICA

PASSBOOK® SERIES

THE *PASSBOOK® SERIES* has been created to prepare applicants and candidates for the ultimate academic battlefield – the examination room.

At some time in our lives, each and every one of us may be required to take an examination – for validation, matriculation, admission, qualification, registration, certification, or licensure.

Based on the assumption that every applicant or candidate has met the basic formal educational standards, has taken the required number of courses, and read the necessary texts, the *PASSBOOK® SERIES* furnishes the one special preparation which may assure passing with confidence, instead of failing with insecurity. Examination questions – together with answers – are furnished as the basic vehicle for study so that the mysteries of the examination and its compounding difficulties may be eliminated or diminished by a sure method.

This book is meant to help you pass your examination provided that you qualify and are serious in your objective.

The entire field is reviewed through the huge store of content information which is succinctly presented through a provocative and challenging approach – the question-and-answer method.

A climate of success is established by furnishing the correct answers at the end of each test.

You soon learn to recognize types of questions, forms of questions, and patterns of questioning. You may even begin to anticipate expected outcomes.

You perceive that many questions are repeated or adapted so that you can gain acute insights, which may enable you to score many sure points.

You learn how to confront new questions, or types of questions, and to attack them confidently and work out the correct answers.

You note objectives and emphases, and recognize pitfalls and dangers, so that you may make positive educational adjustments.

Moreover, you are kept fully informed in relation to new concepts, methods, practices, and directions in the field.

You discover that you are actually taking the examination all the time: you are preparing for the examination by "taking" an examination, not by reading extraneous and/or supererogatory textbooks.

In short, this PASSBOOK®, used directedly, should be an important factor in helping you to pass your test.

FOOD SERVICE WORKER

DUTIES:
As a Food Service Worker, you would be responsible for serving food and for keeping the places where food is served both clean and in good order. This may require medium to heavy physical effort. You would help to prepare trays for serving, transport food carts to serving areas, and return used dishes and equipment to pot and dishwashing areas. You would clean serving or trayline areas as appropriate and make sure that all equipment is ready for the next meal. You would participate in sanitation activities in dining areas and in other food service and preparation areas, order and store supplies, and generally help to insure that individuals in the care of the facility are fed properly; perform related duties.

SCOPE OF EXAMINATION:
The written test will be designed to test for knowledge, skills and/or abilities in such areas as:
1. Food preparation, service, sanitation and storage;
2. Understanding and interpreting written material;
3. Reading gauges, dials and similar instruments; and
4. Arithmetic computation.

HOW TO TAKE A TEST

I. YOU MUST PASS AN EXAMINATION

A. *WHAT EVERY CANDIDATE SHOULD KNOW*

Examination applicants often ask us for help in preparing for the written test. What can I study in advance? What kinds of questions will be asked? How will the test be given? How will the papers be graded?

As an applicant for a civil service examination, you may be wondering about some of these things. Our purpose here is to suggest effective methods of advance study and to describe civil service examinations.

Your chances for success on this examination can be increased if you know how to prepare. Those "pre-examination jitters" can be reduced if you know what to expect. You can even experience an adventure in good citizenship if you know why civil service exams are given.

B. *WHY ARE CIVIL SERVICE EXAMINATIONS GIVEN?*

Civil service examinations are important to you in two ways. As a citizen, you want public jobs filled by employees who know how to do their work. As a job seeker, you want a fair chance to compete for that job on an equal footing with other candidates. The best-known means of accomplishing this two-fold goal is the competitive examination.

Exams are widely publicized throughout the nation. They may be administered for jobs in federal, state, city, municipal, town or village governments or agencies.

Any citizen may apply, with some limitations, such as the age or residence of applicants. Your experience and education may be reviewed to see whether you meet the requirements for the particular examination. When these requirements exist, they are reasonable and applied consistently to all applicants. Thus, a competitive examination may cause you some uneasiness now, but it is your privilege and safeguard.

C. *HOW ARE CIVIL SERVICE EXAMS DEVELOPED?*

Examinations are carefully written by trained technicians who are specialists in the field known as "psychological measurement," in consultation with recognized authorities in the field of work that the test will cover. These experts recommend the subject matter areas or skills to be tested; only those knowledges or skills important to your success on the job are included. The most reliable books and source materials available are used as references. Together, the experts and technicians judge the difficulty level of the questions.

Test technicians know how to phrase questions so that the problem is clearly stated. Their ethics do not permit "trick" or "catch" questions. Questions may have been tried out on sample groups, or subjected to statistical analysis, to determine their usefulness.

Written tests are often used in combination with performance tests, ratings of training and experience, and oral interviews. All of these measures combine to form the best-known means of finding the right person for the right job.

II. HOW TO PASS THE WRITTEN TEST

A. NATURE OF THE EXAMINATION

To prepare intelligently for civil service examinations, you should know how they differ from school examinations you have taken. In school you were assigned certain definite pages to read or subjects to cover. The examination questions were quite detailed and usually emphasized memory. Civil service exams, on the other hand, try to discover your present ability to perform the duties of a position, plus your potentiality to learn these duties. In other words, a civil service exam attempts to predict how successful you will be. Questions cover such a broad area that they cannot be as minute and detailed as school exam questions.

In the public service similar kinds of work, or positions, are grouped together in one "class." This process is known as *position-classification*. All the positions in a class are paid according to the salary range for that class. One class title covers all of these positions, and they are all tested by the same examination.

B. FOUR BASIC STEPS

1) Study the announcement

How, then, can you know what subjects to study? Our best answer is: "Learn as much as possible about the class of positions for which you've applied." The exam will test the knowledge, skills and abilities needed to do the work.

Your most valuable source of information about the position you want is the official exam announcement. This announcement lists the training and experience qualifications. Check these standards and apply only if you come reasonably close to meeting them.

The brief description of the position in the examination announcement offers some clues to the subjects which will be tested. Think about the job itself. Review the duties in your mind. Can you perform them, or are there some in which you are rusty? Fill in the blank spots in your preparation.

Many jurisdictions preview the written test in the exam announcement by including a section called "Knowledge and Abilities Required," "Scope of the Examination," or some similar heading. Here you will find out specifically what fields will be tested.

2) Review your own background

Once you learn in general what the position is all about, and what you need to know to do the work, ask yourself which subjects you already know fairly well and which need improvement. You may wonder whether to concentrate on improving your strong areas or on building some background in your fields of weakness. When the announcement has specified "some knowledge" or "considerable knowledge," or has used adjectives like "beginning principles of..." or "advanced ... methods," you can get a clue as to the number and difficulty of questions to be asked in any given field. More questions, and hence broader coverage, would be included for those subjects which are more important in the work. Now weigh your strengths and weaknesses against the job requirements and prepare accordingly.

3) Determine the level of the position

Another way to tell how intensively you should prepare is to understand the level of the job for which you are applying. Is it the entering level? In other words, is this the position in which beginners in a field of work are hired? Or is it an intermediate or advanced level? Sometimes this is indicated by such words as "Junior" or "Senior" in the class title. Other jurisdictions use Roman numerals to designate the level – Clerk I, Clerk II, for example. The word "Supervisor" sometimes appears in the title. If the level is not indicated by the title, check the description of duties. Will you be working under very close supervision, or will you have responsibility for independent decisions in this work?

4) Choose appropriate study materials

Now that you know the subjects to be examined and the relative amount of each subject to be covered, you can choose suitable study materials. For beginning level jobs, or even advanced ones, if you have a pronounced weakness in some aspect of your training, read a modern, standard textbook in that field. Be sure it is up to date and has general coverage. Such books are normally available at your library, and the librarian will be glad to help you locate one. For entry-level positions, questions of appropriate difficulty are chosen -- neither highly advanced questions, nor those too simple. Such questions require careful thought but not advanced training.

If the position for which you are applying is technical or advanced, you will read more advanced, specialized material. If you are already familiar with the basic principles of your field, elementary textbooks would waste your time. Concentrate on advanced textbooks and technical periodicals. Think through the concepts and review difficult problems in your field.

These are all general sources. You can get more ideas on your own initiative, following these leads. For example, training manuals and publications of the government agency which employs workers in your field can be useful, particularly for technical and professional positions. A letter or visit to the government department involved may result in more specific study suggestions, and certainly will provide you with a more definite idea of the exact nature of the position you are seeking.

III. KINDS OF TESTS

Tests are used for purposes other than measuring knowledge and ability to perform specified duties. For some positions, it is equally important to test ability to make adjustments to new situations or to profit from training. In others, basic mental abilities not dependent on information are essential. Questions which test these things may not appear as pertinent to the duties of the position as those which test for knowledge and information. Yet they are often highly important parts of a fair examination. For very general questions, it is almost impossible to help you direct your study efforts. What we can do is to point out some of the more common of these general abilities needed in public service positions and describe some typical questions.

1) General information

Broad, general information has been found useful for predicting job success in some kinds of work. This is tested in a variety of ways, from vocabulary lists to questions about current events. Basic background in some field of work, such as sociology or economics, may be sampled in a group of questions. Often these are principles which have become familiar to most persons through exposure rather than through formal training. It is difficult to advise you how to study for these questions; being alert to the world around you is our best suggestion.

2) Verbal ability

An example of an ability needed in many positions is verbal or language ability. Verbal ability is, in brief, the ability to use and understand words. Vocabulary and grammar tests are typical measures of this ability. Reading comprehension or paragraph interpretation questions are common in many kinds of civil service tests. You are given a paragraph of written material and asked to find its central meaning.

3) Numerical ability

Number skills can be tested by the familiar arithmetic problem, by checking paired lists of numbers to see which are alike and which are different, or by interpreting charts and graphs. In the latter test, a graph may be printed in the test booklet which you are asked to use as the basis for answering questions.

4) Observation

A popular test for law-enforcement positions is the observation test. A picture is shown to you for several minutes, then taken away. Questions about the picture test your ability to observe both details and larger elements.

5) Following directions

In many positions in the public service, the employee must be able to carry out written instructions dependably and accurately. You may be given a chart with several columns, each column listing a variety of information. The questions require you to carry out directions involving the information given in the chart.

6) Skills and aptitudes

Performance tests effectively measure some manual skills and aptitudes. When the skill is one in which you are trained, such as typing or shorthand, you can practice. These tests are often very much like those given in business school or high school courses. For many of the other skills and aptitudes, however, no short-time preparation can be made. Skills and abilities natural to you or that you have developed throughout your lifetime are being tested.

Many of the general questions just described provide all the data needed to answer the questions and ask you to use your reasoning ability to find the answers. Your best preparation for these tests, as well as for tests of facts and ideas, is to be at your physical and mental best. You, no doubt, have your own methods of getting into an exam-taking mood and keeping "in shape." The next section lists some ideas on this subject.

IV. KINDS OF QUESTIONS

Only rarely is the "essay" question, which you answer in narrative form, used in civil service tests. Civil service tests are usually of the short-answer type. Full instructions for answering these questions will be given to you at the examination. But in case this is your first experience with short-answer questions and separate answer sheets, here is what you need to know:

1) Multiple-choice Questions

Most popular of the short-answer questions is the "multiple choice" or "best answer" question. It can be used, for example, to test for factual knowledge, ability to solve problems or judgment in meeting situations found at work.

A multiple-choice question is normally one of three types—
- It can begin with an incomplete statement followed by several possible endings. You are to find the one ending which *best* completes the statement, although some of the others may not be entirely wrong.
- It can also be a complete statement in the form of a question which is answered by choosing one of the statements listed.

- It can be in the form of a problem – again you select the best answer.

Here is an example of a multiple-choice question with a discussion which should give you some clues as to the method for choosing the right answer:

When an employee has a complaint about his assignment, the action which will *best* help him overcome his difficulty is to
- A. discuss his difficulty with his coworkers
- B. take the problem to the head of the organization
- C. take the problem to the person who gave him the assignment
- D. say nothing to anyone about his complaint

In answering this question, you should study each of the choices to find which is best. Consider choice "A" – Certainly an employee may discuss his complaint with fellow employees, but no change or improvement can result, and the complaint remains unresolved. Choice "B" is a poor choice since the head of the organization probably does not know what assignment you have been given, and taking your problem to him is known as "going over the head" of the supervisor. The supervisor, or person who made the assignment, is the person who can clarify it or correct any injustice. Choice "C" is, therefore, correct. To say nothing, as in choice "D," is unwise. Supervisors have and interest in knowing the problems employees are facing, and the employee is seeking a solution to his problem.

2) True/False Questions

The "true/false" or "right/wrong" form of question is sometimes used. Here a complete statement is given. Your job is to decide whether the statement is right or wrong.

SAMPLE: A roaming cell-phone call to a nearby city costs less than a non-roaming call to a distant city.

This statement is wrong, or false, since roaming calls are more expensive.

This is not a complete list of all possible question forms, although most of the others are variations of these common types. You will always get complete directions for answering questions. Be sure you understand *how* to mark your answers – ask questions until you do.

V. RECORDING YOUR ANSWERS

Computer terminals are used more and more today for many different kinds of exams.

For an examination with very few applicants, you may be told to record your answers in the test booklet itself. Separate answer sheets are much more common. If this separate answer sheet is to be scored by machine – and this is often the case – it is highly important that you mark your answers correctly in order to get credit.

An electronic scoring machine is often used in civil service offices because of the speed with which papers can be scored. Machine-scored answer sheets must be marked with a pencil, which will be given to you. This pencil has a high graphite content which responds to the electronic scoring machine. As a matter of fact, stray dots may register as answers, so do not let your pencil rest on the answer sheet while you are pondering the correct answer. Also, if your pencil lead breaks or is otherwise defective, ask for another.

Since the answer sheet will be dropped in a slot in the scoring machine, be careful not to bend the corners or get the paper crumpled.

The answer sheet normally has five vertical columns of numbers, with 30 numbers to a column. These numbers correspond to the question numbers in your test booklet. After each number, going across the page are four or five pairs of dotted lines. These short dotted lines have small letters or numbers above them. The first two pairs may also have a "T" or "F" above the letters. This indicates that the first two pairs only are to be used if the questions are of the true-false type. If the questions are multiple choice, disregard the "T" and "F" and pay attention only to the small letters or numbers.

Answer your questions in the manner of the sample that follows:

32. The largest city in the United States is
    A. Washington, D.C.
    B. New York City
    C. Chicago
    D. Detroit
    E. San Francisco

1) Choose the answer you think is best. (New York City is the largest, so "B" is correct.)
2) Find the row of dotted lines numbered the same as the question you are answering. (Find row number 32)
3) Find the pair of dotted lines corresponding to the answer. (Find the pair of lines under the mark "B.")
4) Make a solid black mark between the dotted lines.

VI. BEFORE THE TEST

Common sense will help you find procedures to follow to get ready for an examination. Too many of us, however, overlook these sensible measures. Indeed, nervousness and fatigue have been found to be the most serious reasons why applicants fail to do their best on civil service tests. Here is a list of reminders:

- Begin your preparation early – Don't wait until the last minute to go scurrying around for books and materials or to find out what the position is all about.
- Prepare continuously – An hour a night for a week is better than an all-night cram session. This has been definitely established. What is more, a night a week for a month will return better dividends than crowding your study into a shorter period of time.
- Locate the place of the exam – You have been sent a notice telling you when and where to report for the examination. If the location is in a different town or otherwise unfamiliar to you, it would be well to inquire the best route and learn something about the building.
- Relax the night before the test – Allow your mind to rest. Do not study at all that night. Plan some mild recreation or diversion; then go to bed early and get a good night's sleep.
- Get up early enough to make a leisurely trip to the place for the test – This way unforeseen events, traffic snarls, unfamiliar buildings, etc. will not upset you.
- Dress comfortably – A written test is not a fashion show. You will be known by number and not by name, so wear something comfortable.

- Leave excess paraphernalia at home – Shopping bags and odd bundles will get in your way. You need bring only the items mentioned in the official notice you received; usually everything you need is provided. Do not bring reference books to the exam. They will only confuse those last minutes and be taken away from you when in the test room.
- Arrive somewhat ahead of time – If because of transportation schedules you must get there very early, bring a newspaper or magazine to take your mind off yourself while waiting.
- Locate the examination room – When you have found the proper room, you will be directed to the seat or part of the room where you will sit. Sometimes you are given a sheet of instructions to read while you are waiting. Do not fill out any forms until you are told to do so; just read them and be prepared.
- Relax and prepare to listen to the instructions
- If you have any physical problem that may keep you from doing your best, be sure to tell the test administrator. If you are sick or in poor health, you really cannot do your best on the exam. You can come back and take the test some other time.

VII. AT THE TEST

The day of the test is here and you have the test booklet in your hand. The temptation to get going is very strong. Caution! There is more to success than knowing the right answers. You must know how to identify your papers and understand variations in the type of short-answer question used in this particular examination. Follow these suggestions for maximum results from your efforts:

1) Cooperate with the monitor

The test administrator has a duty to create a situation in which you can be as much at ease as possible. He will give instructions, tell you when to begin, check to see that you are marking your answer sheet correctly, and so on. He is not there to guard you, although he will see that your competitors do not take unfair advantage. He wants to help you do your best.

2) Listen to all instructions

Don't jump the gun! Wait until you understand all directions. In most civil service tests you get more time than you need to answer the questions. So don't be in a hurry. Read each word of instructions until you clearly understand the meaning. Study the examples, listen to all announcements and follow directions. Ask questions if you do not understand what to do.

3) Identify your papers

Civil service exams are usually identified by number only. You will be assigned a number; you must not put your name on your test papers. Be sure to copy your number correctly. Since more than one exam may be given, copy your exact examination title.

4) Plan your time

Unless you are told that a test is a "speed" or "rate of work" test, speed itself is usually not important. Time enough to answer all the questions will be provided, but this does not mean that you have all day. An overall time limit has been set. Divide the total time (in minutes) by the number of questions to determine the approximate time you have for each question.

5) Do not linger over difficult questions

If you come across a difficult question, mark it with a paper clip (useful to have along) and come back to it when you have been through the booklet. One caution if you do this – be sure to skip a number on your answer sheet as well. Check often to be sure that you have not lost your place and that you are marking in the row numbered the same as the question you are answering.

6) Read the questions

Be sure you know what the question asks! Many capable people are unsuccessful because they failed to *read* the questions correctly.

7) Answer all questions

Unless you have been instructed that a penalty will be deducted for incorrect answers, it is better to guess than to omit a question.

8) Speed tests

It is often better NOT to guess on speed tests. It has been found that on timed tests people are tempted to spend the last few seconds before time is called in marking answers at random – without even reading them – in the hope of picking up a few extra points. To discourage this practice, the instructions may warn you that your score will be "corrected" for guessing. That is, a penalty will be applied. The incorrect answers will be deducted from the correct ones, or some other penalty formula will be used.

9) Review your answers

If you finish before time is called, go back to the questions you guessed or omitted to give them further thought. Review other answers if you have time.

10) Return your test materials

If you are ready to leave before others have finished or time is called, take ALL your materials to the monitor and leave quietly. Never take any test material with you. The monitor can discover whose papers are not complete, and taking a test booklet may be grounds for disqualification.

VIII. EXAMINATION TECHNIQUES

1) Read the general instructions carefully. These are usually printed on the first page of the exam booklet. As a rule, these instructions refer to the timing of the examination; the fact that you should not start work until the signal and must stop work at a signal, etc. If there are any *special* instructions, such as a choice of questions to be answered, make sure that you note this instruction carefully.

2) When you are ready to start work on the examination, that is as soon as the signal has been given, read the instructions to each question booklet, underline any key words or phrases, such as *least, best, outline, describe* and the like. In this way you will tend to answer as requested rather than discover on reviewing your paper that you *listed without describing*, that you selected the *worst* choice rather than the *best* choice, etc.

3) If the examination is of the objective or multiple-choice type – that is, each question will also give a series of possible answers: A, B, C or D, and you are called upon to select the best answer and write the letter next to that answer on your answer paper – it is advisable to start answering each question in turn. There may be anywhere from 50 to 100 such questions in the three or four hours allotted and you can see how much time would be taken if you read through all the questions before beginning to answer any. Furthermore, if you come across a question or group of questions which you know would be difficult to answer, it would undoubtedly affect your handling of all the other questions.

4) If the examination is of the essay type and contains but a few questions, it is a moot point as to whether you should read all the questions before starting to answer any one. Of course, if you are given a choice – say five out of seven and the like – then it is essential to read all the questions so you can eliminate the two that are most difficult. If, however, you are asked to answer all the questions, there may be danger in trying to answer the easiest one first because you may find that you will spend too much time on it. The best technique is to answer the first question, then proceed to the second, etc.

5) Time your answers. Before the exam begins, write down the time it started, then add the time allowed for the examination and write down the time it must be completed, then divide the time available somewhat as follows:
    - If 3-1/2 hours are allowed, that would be 210 minutes. If you have 80 objective-type questions, that would be an average of 2-1/2 minutes per question. Allow yourself no more than 2 minutes per question, or a total of 160 minutes, which will permit about 50 minutes to review.
    - If for the time allotment of 210 minutes there are 7 essay questions to answer, that would average about 30 minutes a question. Give yourself only 25 minutes per question so that you have about 35 minutes to review.

6) The most important instruction is to *read each question* and make sure you know what is wanted. The second most important instruction is to *time yourself properly* so that you answer every question. The third most important instruction is to *answer every question*. Guess if you have to but include something for each question. Remember that you will receive no credit for a blank and will probably receive some credit if you write something in answer to an essay question. If you guess a letter – say "B" for a multiple-choice question – you may have guessed right. If you leave a blank as an answer to a multiple-choice question, the examiners may respect your feelings but it will not add a point to your score. Some exams may penalize you for wrong answers, so in such cases *only*, you may not want to guess unless you have some basis for your answer.

7) Suggestions
    a. Objective-type questions
        1. Examine the question booklet for proper sequence of pages and questions
        2. Read all instructions carefully
        3. Skip any question which seems too difficult; return to it after all other questions have been answered
        4. Apportion your time properly; do not spend too much time on any single question or group of questions

5. Note and underline key words – *all, most, fewest, least, best, worst, same, opposite,* etc.
6. Pay particular attention to negatives
7. Note unusual option, e.g., unduly long, short, complex, different or similar in content to the body of the question
8. Observe the use of "hedging" words – *probably, may, most likely,* etc.
9. Make sure that your answer is put next to the same number as the question
10. Do not second-guess unless you have good reason to believe the second answer is definitely more correct
11. Cross out original answer if you decide another answer is more accurate; do not erase until you are ready to hand your paper in
12. Answer all questions; guess unless instructed otherwise
13. Leave time for review

   b. Essay questions
1. Read each question carefully
2. Determine exactly what is wanted. Underline key words or phrases.
3. Decide on outline or paragraph answer
4. Include many different points and elements unless asked to develop any one or two points or elements
5. Show impartiality by giving pros and cons unless directed to select one side only
6. Make and write down any assumptions you find necessary to answer the questions
7. Watch your English, grammar, punctuation and choice of words
8. Time your answers; don't crowd material

8) Answering the essay question

Most essay questions can be answered by framing the specific response around several key words or ideas. Here are a few such key words or ideas:

M's: manpower, materials, methods, money, management
P's: purpose, program, policy, plan, procedure, practice, problems, pitfalls, personnel, public relations

   a. Six basic steps in handling problems:
1. Preliminary plan and background development
2. Collect information, data and facts
3. Analyze and interpret information, data and facts
4. Analyze and develop solutions as well as make recommendations
5. Prepare report and sell recommendations
6. Install recommendations and follow up effectiveness

   b. Pitfalls to avoid
1. *Taking things for granted* – A statement of the situation does not necessarily imply that each of the elements is necessarily true; for example, a complaint may be invalid and biased so that all that can be taken for granted is that a complaint has been registered

2. *Considering only one side of a situation* – Wherever possible, indicate several alternatives and then point out the reasons you selected the best one
3. *Failing to indicate follow up* – Whenever your answer indicates action on your part, make certain that you will take proper follow-up action to see how successful your recommendations, procedures or actions turn out to be
4. *Taking too long in answering any single question* – Remember to time your answers properly

IX. AFTER THE TEST

Scoring procedures differ in detail among civil service jurisdictions although the general principles are the same. Whether the papers are hand-scored or graded by machine we have described, they are nearly always graded by number. That is, the person who marks the paper knows only the number – never the name – of the applicant. Not until all the papers have been graded will they be matched with names. If other tests, such as training and experience or oral interview ratings have been given, scores will be combined. Different parts of the examination usually have different weights. For example, the written test might count 60 percent of the final grade, and a rating of training and experience 40 percent. In many jurisdictions, veterans will have a certain number of points added to their grades.

After the final grade has been determined, the names are placed in grade order and an eligible list is established. There are various methods for resolving ties between those who get the same final grade – probably the most common is to place first the name of the person whose application was received first. Job offers are made from the eligible list in the order the names appear on it. You will be notified of your grade and your rank as soon as all these computations have been made. This will be done as rapidly as possible.

People who are found to meet the requirements in the announcement are called "eligibles." Their names are put on a list of eligible candidates. An eligible's chances of getting a job depend on how high he stands on this list and how fast agencies are filling jobs from the list.

When a job is to be filled from a list of eligibles, the agency asks for the names of people on the list of eligibles for that job. When the civil service commission receives this request, it sends to the agency the names of the three people highest on this list. Or, if the job to be filled has specialized requirements, the office sends the agency the names of the top three persons who meet these requirements from the general list.

The appointing officer makes a choice from among the three people whose names were sent to him. If the selected person accepts the appointment, the names of the others are put back on the list to be considered for future openings.

That is the rule in hiring from all kinds of eligible lists, whether they are for typist, carpenter, chemist, or something else. For every vacancy, the appointing officer has his choice of any one of the top three eligibles on the list. This explains why the person whose name is on top of the list sometimes does not get an appointment when some of the persons lower on the list do. If the appointing officer chooses the second or third eligible, the No. 1 eligible does not get a job at once, but stays on the list until he is appointed or the list is terminated.

X. HOW TO PASS THE INTERVIEW TEST

The examination for which you applied requires an oral interview test. You have already taken the written test and you are now being called for the interview test – the final part of the formal examination.

You may think that it is not possible to prepare for an interview test and that there are no procedures to follow during an interview. Our purpose is to point out some things you can do in advance that will help you and some good rules to follow and pitfalls to avoid while you are being interviewed.

What is an interview supposed to test?

The written examination is designed to test the technical knowledge and competence of the candidate; the oral is designed to evaluate intangible qualities, not readily measured otherwise, and to establish a list showing the relative fitness of each candidate – as measured against his competitors – for the position sought. Scoring is not on the basis of "right" and "wrong," but on a sliding scale of values ranging from "not passable" to "outstanding." As a matter of fact, it is possible to achieve a relatively low score without a single "incorrect" answer because of evident weakness in the qualities being measured.

Occasionally, an examination may consist entirely of an oral test – either an individual or a group oral. In such cases, information is sought concerning the technical knowledges and abilities of the candidate, since there has been no written examination for this purpose. More commonly, however, an oral test is used to supplement a written examination.

Who conducts interviews?

The composition of oral boards varies among different jurisdictions. In nearly all, a representative of the personnel department serves as chairman. One of the members of the board may be a representative of the department in which the candidate would work. In some cases, "outside experts" are used, and, frequently, a businessman or some other representative of the general public is asked to serve. Labor and management or other special groups may be represented. The aim is to secure the services of experts in the appropriate field.

However the board is composed, it is a good idea (and not at all improper or unethical) to ascertain in advance of the interview who the members are and what groups they represent. When you are introduced to them, you will have some idea of their backgrounds and interests, and at least you will not stutter and stammer over their names.

What should be done before the interview?

While knowledge about the board members is useful and takes some of the surprise element out of the interview, there is other preparation which is more substantive. It *is* possible to prepare for an oral interview – in several ways:

1) Keep a copy of your application and review it carefully before the interview

This may be the only document before the oral board, and the starting point of the interview. Know what education and experience you have listed there, and the sequence and dates of all of it. Sometimes the board will ask you to review the highlights of your experience for them; you should not have to hem and haw doing it.

2) Study the class specification and the examination announcement

Usually, the oral board has one or both of these to guide them. The qualities, characteristics or knowledges required by the position sought are stated in these documents. They offer valuable clues as to the nature of the oral interview. For example, if the job involves supervisory responsibilities, the announcement will usually indicate that knowledge of modern supervisory methods and the qualifications of the candidate as a supervisor will be tested. If so, you can expect such questions, frequently in the form of a hypothetical situation which you are expected to solve. NEVER go into an oral without knowledge of the duties and responsibilities of the job you seek.

3) Think through each qualification required

Try to visualize the kind of questions you would ask if you were a board member. How well could you answer them? Try especially to appraise your own knowledge and background in each area, *measured against the job sought*, and identify any areas in which you are weak. Be critical and realistic – do not flatter yourself.

4) Do some general reading in areas in which you feel you may be weak

For example, if the job involves supervision and your past experience has NOT, some general reading in supervisory methods and practices, particularly in the field of human relations, might be useful. Do NOT study agency procedures or detailed manuals. The oral board will be testing your understanding and capacity, not your memory.

5) Get a good night's sleep and watch your general health and mental attitude

You will want a clear head at the interview. Take care of a cold or any other minor ailment, and of course, no hangovers.

What should be done on the day of the interview?

Now comes the day of the interview itself. Give yourself plenty of time to get there. Plan to arrive somewhat ahead of the scheduled time, particularly if your appointment is in the fore part of the day. If a previous candidate fails to appear, the board might be ready for you a bit early. By early afternoon an oral board is almost invariably behind schedule if there are many candidates, and you may have to wait. Take along a book or magazine to read, or your application to review, but leave any extraneous material in the waiting room when you go in for your interview. In any event, relax and compose yourself.

The matter of dress is important. The board is forming impressions about you – from your experience, your manners, your attitude, and your appearance. Give your personal appearance careful attention. Dress your best, but not your flashiest. Choose conservative, appropriate clothing, and be sure it is immaculate. This is a business interview, and your appearance should indicate that you regard it as such. Besides, being well groomed and properly dressed will help boost your confidence.

Sooner or later, someone will call your name and escort you into the interview room. *This is it.* From here on you are on your own. It is too late for any more preparation. But remember, you asked for this opportunity to prove your fitness, and you are here because your request was granted.

What happens when you go in?

The usual sequence of events will be as follows: The clerk (who is often the board stenographer) will introduce you to the chairman of the oral board, who will introduce you to the other members of the board. Acknowledge the introductions before you sit down. Do not be surprised if you find a microphone facing you or a stenotypist sitting by. Oral interviews are usually recorded in the event of an appeal or other review.

Usually the chairman of the board will open the interview by reviewing the highlights of your education and work experience from your application – primarily for the benefit of the other members of the board, as well as to get the material into the record. Do not interrupt or comment unless there is an error or significant misinterpretation; if that is the case, do not hesitate. But do not quibble about insignificant matters. Also, he will usually ask you some question about your education, experience or your present job – partly to get you to start talking and to establish the interviewing "rapport." He may start the actual questioning, or turn it over to one of the other members. Frequently, each member undertakes the questioning on a particular area, one in which he is perhaps most competent, so you can expect each member to participate in the examination. Because time is limited, you may also expect some rather abrupt switches in the direction the questioning takes, so do not be upset by it. Normally, a board member will not pursue a single line of questioning unless he discovers a particular strength or weakness.

After each member has participated, the chairman will usually ask whether any member has any further questions, then will ask you if you have anything you wish to add. Unless you are expecting this question, it may floor you. Worse, it may start you off on an extended, extemporaneous speech. The board is not usually seeking more information. The question is principally to offer you a last opportunity to present further qualifications or to indicate that you have nothing to add. So, if you feel that a significant qualification or characteristic has been overlooked, it is proper to point it out in a sentence or so. Do not compliment the board on the thoroughness of their examination -- they have been sketchy, and you know it. If you wish, merely say, "No thank you, I have nothing further to add." This is a point where you can "talk yourself out" of a good impression or fail to present an important bit of information. Remember, *you close the interview yourself*.

The chairman will then say, "That is all, Mr. _____, thank you." Do not be startled; the interview is over, and quicker than you think. Thank him, gather your belongings and take your leave. Save your sigh of relief for the other side of the door.

How to put your best foot forward

Throughout this entire process, you may feel that the board individually and collectively is trying to pierce your defenses, seek out your hidden weaknesses and embarrass and confuse you. Actually, this is not true. They are obliged to make an appraisal of your qualifications for the job you are seeking, and they want to see you in your best light. Remember, they must interview all candidates and a non-cooperative candidate may become a failure in spite of their best efforts to bring out his qualifications. Here are 15 suggestions that will help you:

1) Be natural – Keep your attitude confident, not cocky

If you are not confident that you can do the job, do not expect the board to be. Do not apologize for your weaknesses, try to bring out your strong points. The board is interested in a positive, not negative, presentation. Cockiness will antagonize any board member and make him wonder if you are covering up a weakness by a false show of strength.

2) Get comfortable, but don't lounge or sprawl

Sit erectly but not stiffly. A careless posture may lead the board to conclude that you are careless in other things, or at least that you are not impressed by the importance of the occasion. Either conclusion is natural, even if incorrect. Do not fuss with your clothing, a pencil or an ashtray. Your hands may occasionally be useful to emphasize a point; do not let them become a point of distraction.

3) Do not wisecrack or make small talk

This is a serious situation, and your attitude should show that you consider it as such. Further, the time of the board is limited – they do not want to waste it, and neither should you.

4) Do not exaggerate your experience or abilities
In the first place, from information in the application or other interviews and sources, the board may know more about you than you think. Secondly, you probably will not get away with it. An experienced board is rather adept at spotting such a situation, so do not take the chance.

5) If you know a board member, do not make a point of it, yet do not hide it
Certainly you are not fooling him, and probably not the other members of the board. Do not try to take advantage of your acquaintanceship – it will probably do you little good.

6) Do not dominate the interview
Let the board do that. They will give you the clues – do not assume that you have to do all the talking. Realize that the board has a number of questions to ask you, and do not try to take up all the interview time by showing off your extensive knowledge of the answer to the first one.

7) Be attentive
You only have 20 minutes or so, and you should keep your attention at its sharpest throughout. When a member is addressing a problem or question to you, give him your undivided attention. Address your reply principally to him, but do not exclude the other board members.

8) Do not interrupt
A board member may be stating a problem for you to analyze. He will ask you a question when the time comes. Let him state the problem, and wait for the question.

9) Make sure you understand the question
Do not try to answer until you are sure what the question is. If it is not clear, restate it in your own words or ask the board member to clarify it for you. However, do not haggle about minor elements.

10) Reply promptly but not hastily
A common entry on oral board rating sheets is "candidate responded readily," or "candidate hesitated in replies." Respond as promptly and quickly as you can, but do not jump to a hasty, ill-considered answer.

11) Do not be peremptory in your answers
A brief answer is proper – but do not fire your answer back. That is a losing game from your point of view. The board member can probably ask questions much faster than you can answer them.

12) Do not try to create the answer you think the board member wants
He is interested in what kind of mind you have and how it works – not in playing games. Furthermore, he can usually spot this practice and will actually grade you down on it.

13) Do not switch sides in your reply merely to agree with a board member
Frequently, a member will take a contrary position merely to draw you out and to see if you are willing and able to defend your point of view. Do not start a debate, yet do not surrender a good position. If a position is worth taking, it is worth defending.

14) Do not be afraid to admit an error in judgment if you are shown to be wrong

The board knows that you are forced to reply without any opportunity for careful consideration. Your answer may be demonstrably wrong. If so, admit it and get on with the interview.

15) Do not dwell at length on your present job

The opening question may relate to your present assignment. Answer the question but do not go into an extended discussion. You are being examined for a *new* job, not your present one. As a matter of fact, try to phrase ALL your answers in terms of the job for which you are being examined.

Basis of Rating

Probably you will forget most of these "do's" and "don'ts" when you walk into the oral interview room. Even remembering them all will not ensure you a passing grade. Perhaps you did not have the qualifications in the first place. But remembering them will help you to put your best foot forward, without treading on the toes of the board members.

Rumor and popular opinion to the contrary notwithstanding, an oral board wants you to make the best appearance possible. They know you are under pressure – but they also want to see how you respond to it as a guide to what your reaction would be under the pressures of the job you seek. They will be influenced by the degree of poise you display, the personal traits you show and the manner in which you respond.

ABOUT THIS BOOK

This book contains tests divided into Examination Sections. Go through each test, answering every question in the margin. We have also attached a sample answer sheet at the back of the book that can be removed and used. At the end of each test look at the answer key and check your answers. On the ones you got wrong, look at the right answer choice and learn. Do not fill in the answers first. Do not memorize the questions and answers, but understand the answer and principles involved. On your test, the questions will likely be different from the samples. Questions are changed and new ones added. If you understand these past questions you should have success with any changes that arise. Tests may consist of several types of questions. We have additional books on each subject should more study be advisable or necessary for you. Finally, the more you study, the better prepared you will be. This book is intended to be the last thing you study before you walk into the examination room. Prior study of relevant texts is also recommended. NLC publishes some of these in our Fundamental Series. Knowledge and good sense are important factors in passing your exam. Good luck also helps. So now study this Passbook, absorb the material contained within and take that knowledge into the examination. Then do your best to pass that exam.

EXAMINATION SECTION

EXAMINATION SECTION
TEST 1

DIRECTIONS: Each question or incomplete statement is followed by several suggested answers or completions. Select the one that BEST answers the question or completes the statement. *PRINT THE LETTER OF THE CORRECT ANSWER IN THE SPACE AT THE RIGHT.*

1. Of the following, the requisition which is CORRECT for the number of servings indicated is

    A. 300 lbs. eviscerated frozen turkey for 480 servings
    B. 190 lbs. cured ham, bone in, for ham steaks for 600 servilngs
    C. 100 lbs. whole beef liver for 520 servings
    D. 380 lbs. veal leg, bone in, for roast veal for 500 servings

    1.____

2. Of the following, the LEAST effective way of effecting portion control is by means of

    A. instruction of personnel responsible for serving food
    B. purchase of pre-portioned foods
    C. use of standardized serving utensils
    D. preparation and use of standardized recipes

    2.____

3. The MOST important reason for using a manual in a dietary department is that it serves as a

    A. means of preventing duplication of work
    B. tool for achieving orderly operations
    C. system for controlling food waste
    D. system for controlling food costs

    3.____

4. Of the following, the MOST important reason for using standardized recipes is that they provide

    A. uniformity of quality and quantity of the product
    B. greater control of raw food costs
    C. saving of labor hours resulting in lower cost
    D. guidance in pre-planning of menus

    4.____

5. From the standpoint of the dietitian, the CHIEF advantage of centralized as compared to decentralized food service is that

    A. space needed for floor pantries in a decentralized service can be used instead for other purposes
    B. better controls can be exercised by the dietitian
    C. less service is required from the nursing department
    D. it eliminates complaints that pantry noises on the floor disturb the patients

    5.____

6. Assume that the dishwashing load is unusually heavy for the facilities provided. Of the following, the MOST expedient method for reducing the load would be to

    A. stagger the meal hours
    B. use paper cups for beverages

    6.____

C. increase the number of employees handling the operation
D. decrease the timing on the machine wash and rinse operations

7. The amount of freezer space necessary in a kitchen will depend MAINLY upon the

   A. frequency of delivery service
   B. amount of money that can be tied up in stored items
   C. number of frozen foods used on the menu
   D. savings effected in purchasing in bulk at advantageous times

8. Before recommending a time-saving device, the MOST important factor to be considered is

   A. whether it will be used frequently
   B. the amount of maintenance which will be required
   C. the number of productive labor hours which will be saved
   D. the space it will require

9. Before planning a kitchen layout, it is MOST important to know

   A. how much money will be available
   B. the relation of the kitchen to other areas
   C. the numbers and availability of personnel
   D. what types of menus and service will be used

10. Kitchen equipment should be placed PRIMARILY to

    A. provide neat, uncluttered appearance
    B. avoid cross traffic
    C. permit easy access to the main delivery area
    D. establish a separate work area for each cook

11. The MAIN advantage of using standardized pans is that

    A. the same pan can be used for cooking, serving, and storing
    B. fewer pans are required
    C. they stack better and require less storage space
    D. less time is used to select the right pan for the job

12. Specific cleaning agents and detergents have been recommended for use on various surface materials in order to do a thorough job of cleaning and to maintain the attractive appearance of the material.
    Of the following, the one which you would recommend for the purpose indicated is

    A. tri-sodium phosphate for cleaning aluminum pots and pans
    B. a scouring cleanser with a high percent of abrasive material for cleaning stainless steel tables and trucks
    C. a lye base liquid soap for use in automatic dishwashing machines
    D. a non-oil base detergent for floors covered with light-colored rubber tile

13. Scraping and prerinsing of dishes before running them through the dishwashing machine is necessary to

A. shorten the time of the washing process
B. reduce the amount of detergent needed
C. prevent blocking of the nozzles in the rinse arm of the machine
D. remove food particles which harden at the wash temperature

14. When purchasing food, the one of the following which should be the deciding factor for determining what is the MOST economical buy is the

    A. unit price as purchased
    B. cost of edible portion
    C. cost of product as served
    D. preparation costs

14.____

15. When ordering perishable foods, the specification should designate the condition of the foods as of the time of

    A. delivery   B. shipment   C. packaging   D. bidding

15.____

16. Of the following forms in which meat can be purchased, the form which makes possible MOST accurate portion control is

    A. quarters   B. prefabricated
    C. carcass   D. wholesale cuts

16.____

17. Fresh fruits are generally at their best during certain periods.
    Of the following, the statement which is LEAST accurate is that

    A. cherries are best in June and July
    B. cranberries are best from April to September
    C. grapefruit is best from November to February
    D. California grapes are best from November to February

17.____

18. When labor is the MOST important consideration, it is BEST to purchase potatoes

    A. whole, unpeeled   B. whole, peeled
    C. instant, powdered   D. canned

18.____

19. When purchasing grapefruit for an institution, it is BEST to purchase by the

    A. pound   B. dozen   C. bushel   D. crate count

19.____

20. Of the following, the specification which is LEAST desirable when purchasing fresh vegetables is

    A. cauliflower, leaves trimmed to within 1" to 2" from head
    B. beets, stems completely removed
    C. carrots, topped, tops cut back to less than 1"
    D. celery, stalk length 16" and well trimmed

20.____

21. When accepting a delivery of a large order of frozen foods, it is MOST important to

    A. be sure that the grade which was ordered is received
    B. see that the labels are intact
    C. check for evidence of defrosting
    D. weigh the merchandise to be sure of correct weight

21.____

22. For proper storage of dry and canned food supplies, it is NOT advisable to

    A. place all shelving and stacks close against the wall to prevent falling
    B. stack like items together to facilitate issuing and taking of inventories
    C. store canned goods on shelves or on platforms 4 to 6" off the floor
    D. stack the most recent receipts in back or on the bottom to make the *first in, first out* rule easy to follow

23. If a high bacteria count on the dishes is found in one of the serving units, it is LEAST important to

    A. check the wash and rinse temperature of the dishwashing machine
    B. check the technique for scraping, prerinsing, washing, and rinsing dishes
    C. inspect the serving unit, including all equipment, for cleanliness
    D. arrange for a physical examination of every employee in the department

24. Rodent control is of prime importance in maintaining sanitary conditions. The MOST effective way to eliminate rodents is by

    A. providing regular visits of licensed exterminators
    B. use of traps baited with food
    C. cautious use of rat poisons
    D. elimination of harborages

25. The recommended daily dietary allowance of protein for an aged man is MOST NEARLY _____ gm. per kg. body weight.

    A. .5   B. 1   C. 1.5   D. 2

KEY (CORRECT ANSWERS)

1. A		11. A	
2. A		12. D	
3. B		13. D	
4. A		14. C	
5. B		15. A	
6. B		16. B	
7. A		17. B	
8. C		18. C	
9. D		19. D	
10. B		20. B	

21. C
22. A
23. D
24. D
25. B

TEST 2

DIRECTIONS: Each question or incomplete statement is followed by several suggested answers or completions. Select the one that BEST answers the question or completes the statement. *PRINT THE LETTER OF THE CORRECT ANSWER IN THE SPACE AT THE RIGHT.*

1. The GREATEST amount of protein per unit of body weight is needed during 1.____
   A. childhood   B. infancy   C. adolescence   D. pregnancy

2. The thiamine needs of the individual are dependent upon the 2.____
   A. total caloric intake   B. body weight
   C. body height   D. age

3. Of the following foods, the BEST source of riboflavin is 3.____
   A. lean meat   B. egg   C. milk   D. orange

4. Of the following groups of foods, the one which contains the LARGEST number of alkaline-ash foods is 4.____
   A. milk, sugar, and starch
   B. milk, meat, and potatoes
   C. all fruits and vegetables
   D. most fruits, most vegetables, and milk

5. Of the following nutrients, the one which may reduce the amount of radioactive strontium 90 which may be deposited in the body is 5.____
   A. vitamin D   B. calcium
   C. oleic acid   D. ascorbic acid

6. If taken in massive doses over a period of time, the vitamin which may cause toxic effects is 6.____
   A. ascorbic acid   B. pantothenic acid
   C. vitamin B_{12} D. vitamin A

7. The vitamin which contains cobalt is 7.____
   A. vitamin B_{12} B. folic acid
   C. ascorbic acid   D. riboflavin

8. The term *niacin equivalents* refers to 8.____
   A. foods which have an equivalent niacin content
   B. the increase necessary when metabolism is accelerated
   C. the quantitative tryptophan-niacin relationship
   D. the minimum amount of niacin which will protect against symptoms of pellagra

9. The blood cholesterol level is MOST affected by 9.____
   A. body cholesterol synthesis   B. ingestion of egg yolks
   C. total dietary cholesterol intake   D. total fat intake

10. The calcium is unavailable because it forms an insoluble salt in combination with oxalic acid in

    A. collards   B. carrots   C. beets   D. spinach

11. Following convalescence from gastric surgery, a relatively high proportion of patients experience distressing symptoms after eating.
The diet prescription for this condition is USUALLY

    A. high protein, high fat, low carbohydrate
    B. high protein, low fat, low carbohydrate
    C. high protein, high carbohydrate, low fat
    D. low protein, low fat, high carbohydrate

12. An increase of high residue foods in the diet is indicated in cases of

    A. spastic constipation   B. ulcerative colitis
    C. atonic constipation   D. diverticulitis

13. The dietary treatment for diseases of the liver consists of

    A. high protein, high carbohydrate, and moderate fat intake
    B. moderate protein, low carbohydrate, and low fat intake
    C. high protein, moderate carbohydrate, and moderate fat intake
    D. moderate protein, high carbohydrate, and low fat intake

14. The diet USUALLY prescribed for persons with hyperchlorhydria is _____ diet.

    A. 100 mg. sodium   B. low residue
    C. low phosphorus   D. low purine

15. In the treatment of phenylketonuria, the diet MUST be modified so that

    A. all protein is eliminated from the diet
    B. phenylalanine is completely eliminated from the diet until the child is 5 years old
    C. the serum level of phenylalanine is maintained within normal limits
    D. milk and milk products are the only foods eliminated from the diet

16. When signs of impending hepatic coma appear in a patient with advanced cirrhosis, the diet MOST likely to be ordered is

    A. low protein   B. low carbohydrate
    C. low caloric   D. fat free

17. The one of the following menus which would be BEST to serve to an ulcer patient who follows kosher food laws is

    A. cream of pea soup, cream cheese sandwich, asparagus tips, custard, milk
    B. cream of pea soup, chicken, mashed potatoes, diced carrots, canned pears, milk
    C. tomato juice, beef pattie, baked potato with butter, peas, junket, milk
    D. apple juice, creamed diced shrimp on rice, peas, canned peaches, milk

18. In the treatment of gout, the one of the following which MUST often be restricted because it may inhibit the excretion of uric acid is

    A. carbohydrate
    B. fats
    C. fluids
    D. calcium

19. Of the following groups of foods, the one which may be indicated in a gluten-free diet is

    A. rye, barley, and macaroni
    B. crackers, spaghetti, and rice
    C. cream of wheat, cornstarch, and oats
    D. corn, potato, and rice

20. The one of the following which would NOT alleviate the symptoms of the dumping syndrome is

    A. small frequent feedings instead of large meals
    B. dry meals with fluids taken only between meals
    C. emphasis on concentrated forms of carbohydrates
    D. avoidance of chilled foods

21. The one of the following symptoms which is MOST indicative of riboflavin deficiency is

    A. poor wound healing
    B. fissures at the corners of the mouth
    C. bone deformities
    D. simple goiter

22. A preschool child who is allowed to drink as much as 2 quarts of milk daily to the exclusion of adequate amounts of solid foods is MOST likely to be deficient in

    A. protein   B. riboflavin   C. iron   D. vitamin A

23. The ketosis which occurs in uncontrolled diabetes is caused by the excessive oxidation of

    A. B-complex vitamins
    B. fats
    C. carbohydrates
    D. ascorbic acid

24. *Hidden hunger* may be the result of a diet lacking in sufficient amounts of

    A. foods high in cellulose
    B. high calorie foods
    C. protein foods
    D. protective foods

25. A possible result of protein deficiency is

    A. edema
    B. heart disease
    C. gout
    D. sprue

KEY (CORRECT ANSWERS)

1. B
2. A
3. C
4. D
5. B

6. D
7. A
8. C
9. A
10. D

11. A
12. C
13. A
14. B
15. C

16. A
17. A
18. B
19. D
20. C

21. B
22. C
23. B
24. D
25. A

TEST 3

DIRECTIONS: Each question or incomplete statement is followed by several suggested answers or completions. Select the one that BEST answers the question or completes the statement. *PRINT THE LETTER OF THE CORRECT ANSWER IN THE SPACE AT THE RIGHT.*

1. A negative nitrogen balance occurs when   1._____

    A. more nitrogen is being ingested than is excreted in the urine
    B. new tissue is being built in periods of rapid growth
    C. dietary protein intake is adequate for tissue synthesis
    D. the body's energy needs must be met from the body's stores of fat and the reserves of protein

2. When planning a diet for an overweight adolescent girl, it is MOST important to consider that   2._____

    A. the chief problem is controlling the intake of candy and rich desserts
    B. overweight often disappears by the end of the adolescent period
    C. most problems of overweight are glandular in origin
    D. emotional and social problems are often related to the obesity

3. If a patient with a long-term illness has anorexia, it is MOST important that   3._____

    A. he lie down for a half hour before each meal
    B. he be served his favorite foods first
    C. his nutritional requirements be met in spite of his lack of appetite
    D. he be allowed an alcoholic beverage as an appetite stimulant

4. Assume that the bakers have been scheduled to be off duty on Saturday and Sunday. Under these circumstances, the MOST suitable one of the following combinations of desserts for Sunday is   4._____

    A. brownie a la mode for dinner; cheesecake (frozen) for supper
    B. apple pie a la mode for dinner; baked bread pudding for supper
    C. butterscotch pie for dinner; canned fruit cocktail with cookies for supper
    D. cherry jello with sliced bananas for dinner; Napoleons for supper

5. To increase consumer satisfaction, it is recommended that whenever possible a choice of menu items be offered.   5._____
   Of the following, the choice of menu items which is LEAST appropriate for use in a hospital cafeteria is

    A. stewed prunes or fresh frozen orange juice
    B. half grapefruit or canned applesauce
    C. sliced bananas or baked applies
    D. pineapple juice or grapefruit sections

6. When preparing the menu, it is important to consider ease in serving, overall economy, and utilization of manpower and supplies.
   Of the following menu items, the combination which is LEAST appropriate for a hospital menu is

   A. sliced tomato salad or head lettuce salad
   B. carrot and raisin salad or Waldorf salad
   C. coleslaw or celery and carrot sticks
   D. marinated sliced cucumbers or tossed salad greens

7. Of the following, the one which BEST illustrates the principles of good menu planning is

   A. beef stew, creamed diced potatoes, mixed vegetable salad, bread, butter, chilled fruit cup, coffee, tea or milk
   B. baked stuffed pork chop, mashed potatoes, buttered broccoli, spiced applesauce, bread, butter, raspberry sherbet with vanilla cookies, coffee, tea or milk
   C. French fried shrimp, baked potato, fried eggplant, lettuce salad with Thousand Islands dressing, bread, butter, sugared doughnuts, coffee, tea or milk
   D. cream of celery soup, baked filet of sole, steamed diced potatoes, buttered cauliflower, bread, butter, lemon sherbet, coffee, tea or milk

8. Assume that a disaster has occurred and you have no gas or electricity in your hospital but you have steam and hot water. The feeding census has doubled to 3000.
   The BEST of the following menus to serve under these circumstances is:

   A. steamed frankfurters, Creole lima beans, pickle slices, bread or rolls, butter, mustard, sliced pineapple, boxed cookies, coffee and milk
   B. cold cuts, potato salad, sliced tomatoes, bread, butter, mustard, fresh apples, coffee, milk
   C. tomato juice, hamburgers on a bun, sliced onion, coleslaw, potato chips, canned applesauce, coffee, milk
   D. egg salad on lettuce, baked potato, bread, butter, hot cocoa, canned fruit cocktail

9. The timing of the cooking of fresh and frozen vegetables must be carefully planned into each day's operation if the final product is to be of top quality when it is served. When cooking vegetables in a steam kettle, the vegetables are added after the water comes to a boil and timing begins when the water reboils.
   Of the following, the one which would NOT result in a top quality product is cooking of twenty pounds of

   A. fresh broccoli for 15 to 20 minutes
   B. frozen peas for 25 to 30 minutes
   C. fresh asparagus for 5 to 10 minutes
   D. frozen chopped spinach for 10 to 15 minutes

10. Advance preparation enables the dietary department to serve a variety of menu items not otherwise possible.
    The one of the following items which may be prepared 12 to 24 hours in advance without loss in quality is

    A. Brown Betty   B. stuffed pork chops
    C. potato salad   D. spiced pears

11. When the butcher is instructed to process meat for beef stew, he should be instructed to use beef _____ and beef _____.   11._____

    A. chuck; neck
    B. loin; chuck
    C. round; ribs
    D. neck; loin

12. Of the following, the food items which are NOT interchangeable in recipes are   12._____

    A. chocolate with cocoa and fat
    B. fresh whole milk with non-fat dry milk solids and fat plus water
    C. baking powder with buttermilk and soda
    D. hard flour with soft flour and cornstarch

13. To produce the BEST medium white sauce, you should add for each cup of milk _____ of flour.   13._____

    A. 1 teaspoon
    B. 2 tablespoons
    C. 1/4 cup
    D. 8 tablespoons

14. The quality of food when served is greatly affected by the timing of preparation and cooking.   14._____
    The one of the following which is MOST likely to be of acceptable quality when served is

    A. corn on the cob husked in the morning, refrigerated in plastic bags until 3:30, and cooked for 25 minutes at 4 P.M. for evening meal hour 4:30 to 6 P.M.
    B. hamburgers made from beef freshly ground at 7 A.M., seasoned, shaped and panned at 9 A.M., cooked in oven at 10:30 A.M., and distributed to all dining rooms at 11:30 for noon service until 1 P.M.
    C. baked potatoes, sorted and washed the day before, panned at 7 A.M., placed in hot oven to bake at 20 minute intervals starting at 10:30 A.M., removed at same intervals starting at 11:15 A.M., pierced and sent to dining rooms for service starting at 11:30 A.M.
    D. jelly omelet made by skillet method by cracking eggs early in morning, frying omelets at 10:30 A.M., spreading and folding jelly into them, cutting into standard portions, and placing them in a warm oven to hold for serving at 11:30 to 1 P.M.

15. Of the following, the LEAST important consideration in planning menus is the   15._____

    A. facilities and equipment available for food preparation
    B. ethnic and cultural food habits of patients
    C. per capita budgetary allowance
    D. method of food service to be used

16. In planning alternate choices of food items on a selective menu, it is MOST important to list alternatives which are of approximately the same   16._____

    A. cost per portion
    B. food grouping
    C. degree of acceptability
    D. color and texture

17. Many hospitals favor the use of cycle menus to improve their food service. However, cycle menus should NOT be used to   17._____

    A. simplify menu writing
    B. promote standardization of recipes and food production procedures

C. provide a fixed, unalterable menu pattern
D. help maintain better cost control

18. The one of the following which is LEAST useful in computing raw food costs for a given period is the

    A. inventory records of foods received and issued
    B. unit and total costs of foods used
    C. records of overhead and salaries
    D. record of meals served

18.____

19. The one of the following which has LEAST value in pre-costing a menu before it is served is the

    A. desired portion size of each item
    B. cost of the ingredients
    C. cost of labor
    D. estimated number of portions required

19.____

20. When planning menus, one should try to include items which are generally acceptable to as many individuals as possible to reduce leftovers.
    Of the following, the food you should plan to use LEAST often in order to avoid excessive leftovers is

    A. chicken a la king   B. roast beef
    C. lettuce and tomato salad   D. chocolate layer cake

20.____

21. To maintain good standards of nutrition, the LARGEST percentage of the food dollar should be spent for

    A. cereal products   B. fruits and vegetables
    C. dairy products   D. meats

21.____

22. When giving diet instruction to a patient, the FIRST thing a dietitian should do is to

    A. explain the essentials of an adequate diet
    B. determine the amount of money available for food
    C. determine present and previous patterns of eating
    D. explain that a change in food habits will make the patient healthier

22.____

23. Assume that an older person asks for advice on how he can achieve greater enjoyment of meals and less distress after eating.
    Of the following, the suggestion you should NOT make is that he eat

    A. a good breakfast to start the day
    B. four or five light meals instead of three heavier meals
    C. mostly cereal products since these are easiest to prepare and masticate
    D. the heaviest meal at noon rather than at night if sleeping is difficult

23.____

24. Of the following, the MOST desirable dinner menu for a geriatric patient who is on a regular diet is

    A. grilled frankfurters, baked beans, cole slaw, baked apple
    B. pot roast, noodles, carrot timbale, applesauce

24.____

C. fried chicken, mashed potatoes, rutabagas, cheese strudel
D. broiled fish, French fried potatoes, broccoli, cherry pie

25. Of the following menus, the one which is LEAST acceptable from the point of view of good menu planning for a patient on a regular diet is   25.____

   A. roast lamb, mashed potatoes, buttered carrot rings, applesauce, bread and butter, cottage pudding with custard sauce, coffee, tea or milk
   B. simmered corned beef, parsley buttered potatoes, steamed cabbage wedge, horseradish and beet relish, bread and butter, fresh fruit cup, coffee, tea, milk
   C. Salisbury steak with mushroom gravy, French fried potatoes, sliced tomato salad on chicory, French dressing, vanilla ice cream, oatmeal cookie, coffee, tea, milk
   D. baked cured ham with mustard sauce, scalloped sweet potatoes with apples, cole slaw, bread and butter, Boston cream pie, coffee, tea, milk

KEY (CORRECT ANSWERS)

1.	D	11.	A
2.	D	12.	D
3.	C	13.	B
4.	A	14.	C
5.	C	15.	D
6.	B	16.	B
7.	B	17.	C
8.	A	18.	C
9.	B	19.	D
10.	D	20.	A

21. D
22. C
23. C
24. B
25. A

EXAMINATION SECTION
TEST 1

DIRECTIONS: Each question or incomplete statement is followed by several suggested answers or completions. Select the one that BEST answers the question or completes the statement. *PRINT THE LETTER OF THE CORRECT ANSWER IN THE SPACE AT THE RIGHT.*

1. The one of the following groups of garnishes or accompaniments which is MOST appropriate for the entree designated is   1.____

   A. boiled beef; horseradish sour cream sauce, mixed pickles, beet and onion relish, lemon wedge
   B. roast veal; cranberry sauce, fried apple ring, parsley, French fried onion ring
   C. broiled fish; lemon wedge, tartar sauce, chopped parsley, lemon butter
   D. hamburger; sliced onion, catsup, French fried onion rings, Hollandaise sauce

2. Assume that the following menu has been submitted: chicken fricasee, mashed potatoes, cauliflower, bread and butter, applesauce, coffee, tea, milk.   2.____
   The CHIEF defect of this menu is that it is

   A. inadequate in protein content
   B. lacking in color and texture contrast
   C. improperly balanced as to nutrient content
   D. too high in calories

3. Assume that the following menu has been submitted for lunch: baked ham, pan browned parsnips, baked sweet potato, cornbread and butter, Apple Brown Betty with whipped topping.   3.____
   This menu is NOT well-planned primarily because

   A. there are too many calories
   B. there are no vitamin C foods
   C. there is not enough variety in texture of the foods
   D. the workload is not well distributed for the kitchen's cooking equipment

4. If a patient on a diabetic diet dislikes milk, he may exchange the milk with one   4.____

   A. bread exchange, one meat exchange, and one fat exchange
   B. fruit exchange
   C. bread exchange, one beverage, and one fat exchange
   D. meat exchange and one fruit exchange

5. The one of the following foods which can be used by a diabetic patient as a substitute in a meat exchange is   5.____

   A. ice cream   B. cheddar cheese
   C. lima beans   D. blackeye peas

6. Of the following foods, the one which should NOT be included in a clear liquid diet is   6.____

   A. milk   B. fat-free broth
   C. fruit or vegetable juice   D. carbonated beverages

15

7. The one of the following which is permitted on a 500 mg. sodium diet is

   A. cornflakes
   B. rice krispies
   C. puffed wheat
   D. wheat flakes

8. The one of the following statements which is INCORRECT is that riboflavin

   A. helps the cells utilize oxygen
   B. helps keep vision clear
   C. prevents cracking of mouth corners
   D. helps the body absorb calcium

9. The one of the following which is NOT concerned with the digestion of fat is

   A. cholecystokinin
   B. lipase
   C. bile
   D. ptyalin

10. The diet which should be given to a patient who has chronic kidney disease with nitrogen retention is

    A. high protein, low carbohydrate
    B. low protein
    C. low calcium, low phosphorus
    D. low purine

11. The diet MOST likely to be ordered for the pernicious vomiting of pregnancy is

    A. high carbohydrate, low fat
    B. high carbohydrate, high fat, high protein
    C. low carbohydrate, low fat, high protein
    D. high protein, low sodium

12. In the treatment of hemorrhagic and nutritional anemias, the MOST important nutrients to stress are iron and

    A. protein   B. vitamin A   C. iodine   D. vitamin E

13. The USUAL diet for a patient with acute gallbladder is a _____ diet.

    A. low fat
    B. 1000 mg. sodium
    C. high protein
    D. low cholesterol

14. Assume that a leukemia patient has difficulty swallowing the foods prescribed for her. In order to provide a diet which is nutritionally adequate, it is LEAST advisable to recommend

    A. a liquid diet emphasizing high caloric liquids and protein supplements
    B. nasal tube feeding in order to meet all nutritional requirements and to avoid the problem of swallowing
    C. a diet on which the meat is minced and all fruits and vegetables are pureed
    D. a diet similar to the one prescribed for her except that each item is pureed

15. The diet MOST likely to be prescribed for a patient who has renal stones is a(n) _____ diet.

    A. elimination
    B. low oxalate
    C. low cholesterol
    D. high carbohydrate, low protein, low fat

16. A rice diet is USUALLY prescribed for patients who   16._____

    A. have high blood pressure
    B. have a food allergy
    C. are recovering from a gallbladder operation
    D. require a high caloric intake

17. Patients suffering severe burns are MOST likely to have   17._____

    A. loss of serum protein   B. steatorrhea
    C. polyneuritis   D. stomatitis

18. Of the following statements concerning phenylketonuria, the one that is NOT correct is   18._____
    that it

    A. is caused by an enzyme deficiency
    B. leads to mental retardation
    C. is treated by the restriction of carbohydrates
    D. must be detected in the first few months of life in order to be treated

19. During all periods of growth, vitamin D is essential for efficient absorption and utilization   19._____
    of

    A. calcium and potassium   B. potassium and iron
    C. magnesium and calcium   D. phosphorus and calcium

20. In the treatment of urinary calculi, the one of the following which will assist in maintaining   20._____
    an acid urine is

    A. cranberry juice   B. peas
    C. cabbage   D. corn oil

21. Of the following, the food containing the HIGHEST amount of thiamine per 100 gram por-   21._____
    tion is

    A. fresh green peas   B. fresh pork
    C. fresh spinach   D. ground beef

22. The one of the following foods which is the POOREST source of niacin per 100 gram   22._____
    portion is

    A. lean meats   B. peanuts
    C. whole grain cereals   D. green leafy vegetables

23. Of the following lists of foods, the one which will contribute MOST to the ascorbic acid   23._____
    content of a diet is

    A. potatoes, green peppers, raw cabbage
    B. enriched bread, pork, turnips
    C. whole wheat bread, potatoes, prunes
    D. apples, dates, plums

24. Of the following foods, the content of unsaturated fatty acids is GREATEST in   24._____

    A. butter   B. corn oil
    C. beef suet   D. lard

25. Of the following, the one with the LOWEST vitamin C content per 4 oz. portion is _____ juice. 25.___

    A. orange
    B. lemon
    C. tomato
    D. grapefruit

KEY (CORRECT ANSWERS)

1.	C	11.	A
2.	B	12.	A
3.	D	13.	A
4.	A	14.	C
5.	B	15.	B
6.	A	16.	A
7.	C	17.	A
8.	D	18.	C
9.	D	19.	D
10.	B	20.	A

21. B
22. D
23. A
24. B
25. C

TEST 2

DIRECTIONS: Each question or incomplete statement is followed by several suggested answers or completions. Select the one that BEST answers the question or completes the statement. *PRINT THE LETTER OF THE CORRECT ANSWER IN THE SPACE AT THE RIGHT.*

1. When roasting meat, the GREATEST yield of finished product may be expected when 1.____

    A. it is quickly seared on both sides at the beginning
    B. a high temperature is used throughout the roasting period
    C. a small quantity of water is added during roasting
    D. a low temperature is used throughout the roasting process

2. Of the following, the meat which is LEAST suitable for roasting is 2.____

    A. loin of pork   B. corned brisket
    C. rump of veal   D. leg of lamb

3. The loss of weight which results from braising boneless bottom round of beef, when proper techniques are used, is 3.____

    A. negligible   B. about 10%
    C. about 25%   D. over 50%

4. Of the following, the one which gives the MOST appropriate cooking temperature for the food indicated is 4.____

    A. beef loaf - 450° F   B. baked potatoes - 250° F
    C. caramel custard - 325° F   D. gingerbread - 475° F

5. In teaching a *cook trainee* how to deep fat fry various items of food, one should NOT instruct him to 5.____

    A. lower the food into the fat quickly
    B. make uniform portions of food for frying in the same load
    C. fill frying baskets to no more than 2/3 of capacity
    D. drain raw wet foods well before frying

6. Foods cooked incorrectly often lose flavor.
   When cooking beans or carrots, it is LEAST advisable to 6.____

    A. boil them in a small amount of water
    B. cook them in a steamer
    C. cook them in a pressure cooker
    D. cook them in an uncovered kettle

7. Of the following, the one which would make the LEAST satisfactory thickening agent in a casserole is 7.____

    A. wheat flour   B. rice
    C. cornstarch   D. tapioca

8. If baking powder biscuits do not rise to the proper height, the MOST probable cause is too 8.____

    A. *little* shortening   B. *much* handling of dough
    C. *little* flour   D. *much* baking powder

9. A soggy bottom crust in a lemon meringue pie is MOST probably caused by 9.___

   A. handling the crust too much
   B. baking at too high a temperature
   C. refrigeration of the crust prior to baking
   D. pouring in the filling when the pie is hot

10. The MOST appropriate type of poultry to purchase for chicken a la king is 10.___

    A. fowl   B. roasters   C. fryers   D. broilers

11. Of the following, Grade B eggs may be used MOST satisfactorily for 11.___

    A. poaching   B. scrambling
    C. frying   D. coddling

12. Considering both quality and economy, the BEST choice of the following grades to be 12.___
    specified when ordering apples for sauce is

    A. fancy   B. extra fancy
    C. utility   D. U.S. #1

13. When submitting requisitions, the dietitian should give correct specifications for each 13.___
    item.
    Of the following items, the one which is CORRECTLY specified is

    A. celery - fresh, Grade A, trimmed, in boxes, 140 pounds
    B. oranges - fresh, commercial grade, size 75 to the half crate, 225 pounds
    C. salad greens - romaine, fresh, Grade A, trimmed, 30 pounds
    D. onions - dry, Grade A, in sacks, 200 pounds

14. The one of the following specifications which is INCOMPLETE is 14.___

    A. 200 lbs. of ham, 10 to 12 lbs. each, U.S. #1
    B. 120 lbs. fresh bottom rounds, 20 to 30 lbs. each, Choice
    C. 250 lbs. of boneless corned brisket, deckel removed, 10 to 12 lbs. each, Good
    D. 225 lbs. double veal legs, cut short, 40 to 48 lbs. each, Choice

15. Of the following food items, the one which does NOT have the correct varieties listed for 15.___
    it is

    A. melon - Honeydew, Cantaloupe, Persian, Casaba
    B. potatoes - Idaho, Cobbler, Russet, Yam
    C. onions - Spanish, Bermuda, Yellow, Red
    D. apples - McIntosh, Emperor, Delicious, Concord

16. Assume that you plan to serve 500 portions of beef stew, with 3 ounces of cooked meat 16.___
    in each portion.
    To provide this, you would need _____ lbs. _____ beef chuck.

    A. 95; boneless   B. 100; whole
    C. 125; boneless   D. 175; whole

17. You are serving buttered carrot rings on a menu for which you need 750 servings. 17.____
The number of pounds of topped carrots you should order is MOST NEARLY _____
lbs.

    A. 50   B. 75   C. 150   D. 300

18. Frozen broccoli is on the menu for dinner and you require 260 servings. 18.____
The number of 2 1/2 lb. packages you would need is MOST NEARLY

    A. 10   B. 25   C. 50   D. 100

19. You wish to serve canned peas to 300 patients on the regular diet, 50 patients on bland 19.____
diet, 35 patients on low fat diet, and 65 patients on light diet. Peas are supplied in #10
cans, and these are ordered by the case only.
The number of cases you would need is

    A. 1   B. 2   C. 3   D. 4

20. In order to ensure a minimum of leftover when you plan to serve 3 oz. portions of 20.____
mashed potatoes to 500 persons, it would be BEST to order _____ potatoes.

    A. 40 lbs. instant
    B. 50 lbs. peeled
    C. 2 cases #10 cans of whole
    D. one 100 lb. sack of

21. The one of the following amounts which is MOST likely to yield 100 average servings is 21.____

    A. dry prunes, 25 lbs.
    B. bacon, sliced, rind removed (2 slices per serving), 20 lbs.
    C. coffee, ground for drip, percolator or silex, 2 lbs.
    D. egg noodles, buttered, 18 lbs.

22. The one of the following which would be INCORRECT to order when serving 200 per- 22.____
sons is

    A. 8 #10 cans of applesauce
    B. 1 1/2 cases of #5 cans of tomato juice
    C. 100 lbs. of eviscerated fowl
    D. 20 lbs. of rice

23. To ensure that foods are relatively free of contamination when served in a cafeteria dur- 23.____
ing a three hour meal period, it would be MOST advisable to

    A. stagger periods of preparation and service to the counter
    B. maintain a steam table temperature of 120° F
    C. reheat foods when they cool down
    D. eliminate all creamed foods from the menu

24. If egg salad has been prepared in a safe and sanitary manner, the criterion to be used to 24.____
determine if it may be served one day later is that it

    A. still tastes good
    B. has a satisfactory general appearance
    C. still smells good
    D. has been continuously refrigerated

25. The one of the following statements concerning proper storage which is INCORRECT is that

    A. crates of eggs should be stored upright, never on ends or sides, because eggs are packed with the small end down
    B. crates of lettuce or fruit should not be stacked upright but on the side and should be cross-stacked to provide for air circulation
    C. fresh raw meat such as veal carcass should be carefully wrapped when stored to prevent contamination
    D. onions and potatoes do not require refrigeration; they are best stored in a dark, well-ventilated room at a temperature of 50° to 60° F

25.___

KEY (CORRECT ANSWERS)

1.	D	11.	B
2.	B	12.	C
3.	C	13.	C
4.	C	14.	A
5.	A	15.	D
6.	D	16.	C
7.	C	17.	C
8.	B	18.	B
9.	D	19.	C
10.	A	20.	D

21. C
22. D
23. A
24. D
25. C

TEST 3

DIRECTIONS: Each question or incomplete statement is followed by several suggested answers or completions. Select the one that BEST answers the question or completes the statement. *PRINT THE LETTER OF THE CORRECT ANSWER IN THE SPACE AT THE RIGHT.*

1. Of the following, the one which gives the LEAST desirable temperature for storing the item indicated is 1.____

    A. ripe bananas - 60° to 70° F
    B. fresh eggs - 53° to 58° F
    C. salad greens - 40° to 45° F
    D. fresh lamb - 33° to 38° F

2. Of the following, the MOST important reason for requiring good ventilation in a storeroom is to prevent 2.____

    A. condensation of moisture
    B. roach or rodent infestation
    C. complaints from storekeepers about odors
    D. spoilage of canned goods

3. Of the following foods, the one which is LEAST susceptible to insect infestation is 3.____

    A. dried beans   B. dried fruits
    C. plain gelatin   D. non-fat dry milk

4. Of the following, the MOST effective measure for the elimination of rodents in a hospital kitchen is to 4.____

    A. clean the floors every day
    B. spread poison once a month in all allowable areas
    C. eliminate harborages
    D. screen off the slop sinks at all times

5. Of the following ways to store food, it is LEAST desirable to place 5.____

    A. sacks of dried beans on racks
    B. cans of peas on the floor
    C. packages of cereal on shelves
    D. quarters of lamb on hooks in the refrigerator

6. The MOST important reason for NOT overcrowding refrigerators is to 6.____

    A. make cleaning easier
    B. allow air circulation to reach all foods
    C. prevent waste resulting from overlooked foods
    D. reduce opportunities for pilferage of food

7. Cooked foods should be cooled and refrigerated quickly, PRIMARILY to 7.____

    A. *prevent* growth and development of bacteria
    B. *preserve* food nutrients

23

C. *prevent* loss of moisture content
D. *preserve* a *fresh cooked* appearance

8. In planning the layout of a kitchen, it is MOST important to arrange for

   A. grouping together of large pieces of equipment
   B. a separate work area for each cook
   C. a smooth and orderly flow of work
   D. separation of *wet* and *dry* areas

9. Of the following, the MOST satisfactory work surface for a cook's work table is

   A. hardwood 4" thick
   B. heavy gauge stainless steel
   C. heavy duty galvanized iron
   D. heavy gauge aluminum

10. Of the following, the practice which is LEAST advisable in the operation and maintenance of a food grinder is to

    A. hold the knife and plate in place by screwing the adjustment ring as tight as possible
    B. use a mallet to push pieces of food into the grinder
    C. remove the grinder plate and clean it thoroughly with a brush after each use
    D. remove the grinder head at the end of the day and clean all loose parts before storing them

11. The MAIN reason for selecting a cafeteria counter of standard fabricated units rather than a custom-built counter of the same quality is the

    A. lower initial cost
    B. easier cleaning
    C. greater flexibility for change and expansion
    D. lower maintenance costs

12. Of the following, the MOST suitable steam equipment for a main kitchen in a 100 bed hospital is

    A. one compartment steamer, one 80 gallon jacketed kettle, and one 60 gallon jacketed kettle
    B. two 30 gallon jacketed kettles and one 20 gallon jacketed kettle
    C. one 3 compartment steamer and two 30 gallon jacketed kettles
    D. two 2 compartment steamers and one 20 gallon jacketed kettle

13. The BEST choice for the top of a kitchen work table is

    A. 2 inch solid wood
    B. 12 gauge monel metal
    C. 20 gauge stainless steel
    D. galvanized metal

14. For equipment such as steam tables which require a water supply, it is MOST important to

    A. make sure there are no submerged inlets
    B. specify all stainless steel construction
    C. provide a heat booster
    D. supply both hot and cold water

15. In requisitioning a steam jacketed kettle, the LEAST important specification is that the

    A. draw off tube should be as close to the kettle as possible
    B. bottom should be pitched to facilitate run-off of contents
    C. kettle should be wall hung for easier cleaning
    D. draw off valve should be easily removable

16. The MAIN factor to consider when purchasing a slicing machine is the

    A. ease of cleaning
    B. adequacy of the safety guard for the cutting edge
    C. size of the machine in relation to the volume of slicing
    D. availability of replacement parts

17. In submitting your annual budget, you have requested a 2 drawer work table of complete stainless steel construction.
    If you are told that you must request a less expensive model, the MOST acceptable compromise for you to make would be to

    A. substitute ducoed legs with stainless steel feet
    B. substitute drawers of galvanized metal with stainless steel fronts
    C. specify a lighter weight stainless steel
    D. reduce the size of the table

18. The one of the following which is MOST likely to yield 100 average servings is

    A. fish filet - 30 pounds
    B. cream for coffee - 6 quarts
    C. oatmeal (rolled oats) - 5 pounds
    D. frozen spinach - 10 pounds

19. The one of the following requisitions which is NOT correct for 600 servings is

    A. 15 lbs. of ground coffee
    B. 9 lbs. of margarine chips for toast
    C. 3 #10 cans of jelly
    D. 60 lbs. of granulated sugar for cereal

20. You have requisitioned 8000 lbs. of beef carcass (650 to 700 lbs. per carcass). This will yield tender steaks, tender roasts, and less tender cuts for roasting, stewing, and chopping.
    Taking into account loss from trim, bones, and fat when the carcasses are processed, the amount of edible meat these carcasses should yield is MOST NEARLY _____ lbs.

    A. 4500   B. 5360   C. 6500   D. 7120

21. Analysis of the distribution of the average food dollar in a hospital can be of assistance to the dietitian in planning for and checking on the expenditure of funds.
Of the following, the MOST advisable distribution of funds for categories of food is: meat, poultry, and fish _____%; dairy products _____%; fruits and vegetables _____%; bread and cereal _____%; miscellaneous _____%.

   A. 40; 20; 20; 10; 10
   B. 50; 10; 10; 10; 20
   C. 20; 20; 20; 20; 20
   D. 30; 30; 30; 5; 5

22. When planning a nutrition curriculum for the clinical instruction of student nurses, the factor which deserves the LEAST consideration is the

   A. educational purposes which the school of nursing seeks to attain
   B. educational experiences which are likely to meet the school's objectives
   C. service needs of the dietary department of the hospital
   D. methods of determining if the educational objectives have been attained

23. The current trend in the teaching of nutrition and diet therapy to student nurses emphasizes

   A. role playing and discussion groups as the most significant teaching devices
   B. instruction in food laboratories on preparation of foods
   C. instruction in food preparation and service to patients in the wards
   D. the clinical importance of diet therapy in a patient-centered plan of teaching

24. Suppose that the electric slicer used in the main kitchen is frequently out of order because of a short in the motor. The repair mechanic has demonstrated that this happens because excessive moisture is being used to flush out debris when cleaning the machine.
To prevent repetition of this breakdown, it would be MOST advisable to

   A. issue detailed written instructions on maintenance procedures to all cooks and kitchen employees who might have occasion to use or clean this slicer
   B. issue an order to all employees that no water is to
   C. be used when cleaning this slicer, only clean dry rags
   D. replace the slicer with a manual one that does not have a motor and, therefore, does not require electric current
   E. instruct two employees on each shift on the procedures to be used in cleaning the machine and restrict the use of the machine to them

25. Assume that a dietitian had instructed the kitchen helpers on how to minimize waste when preparing food for cooking. It would be MOST reasonable to conclude that such waste had been reduced subsequently if

   A. on a spot check, the employees observed were preparing the food as instructed
   B. operating costs for the dietary division during the next month were reduced
   C. the amount of food prepared during the next month decreased on a per capita basis
   D. requisitions of food supplies during the next month decreased

KEY (CORRECT ANSWERS)

1. B
2. A
3. C
4. C
5. B

6. B
7. A
8. C
9. B
10. A

11. C
12. C
13. B
14. A
15. C

16. B
17. A
18. A
19. D
20. B

21. A
22. C
23. D
24. D
25. C

EXAMINATION SECTION
TEST 1

DIRECTIONS: Each question or incomplete statement is followed by several suggested answers or completions. Select the one that BEST answers the question or completes the statement. *PRINT THE LETTER OF THE CORRECT ANSWER IN THE SPACE AT THE RIGHT.*

1. The one of the following entrees which offers the LEAST variation in texture is 1.____

    A. turkey, cranberry sauce, fried golden brown potatoes, peas
    B. chopped sirloin, mushroom gravy, French fried potatoes broccoli spears
    C. oven-fried chicken, baked potato, peas and carrots, salad
    D. meat loaf, mashed potatoes, creamed spinach, white bread

2. In planning a menu, the FIRST item which should be chosen is the 2.____

    A. vegetable B. salad C. entree D. dessert

3. Of the following, the BEST method of tenderizing cuts of meat which are less tender is by 3.____

    A. broiling B. stewing C. baking D. deep-frying

4. Which one of the following statements regarding proteins is CORRECT? 4.____

    A. The amount of protein in the body is a constant.
    B. The presence of nitrogen distinguishes protein from carbohydrates and fat.
    C. Protein provides more calories per gram than carbohydrates or fat.
    D. Protein provides the principal source of glucose to brain tissue.

5. The one of the following foods that provides MORE vitamin C per serving than the others is 5.____

    A. brussels sprouts   B. cabbage
    C. tomatoes   D. turnips

6. Liver is a PRIMARY source of which one of the following vitamins? 6.____

    A. A B. B_6 C. C D. D

7. Vitamin A is a fat soluble vitamin essential in an adequate diet for children and adults. Which one of the following statements concerning vitamin A is TRUE? 7.____

    A. The Recommended Daily Allowance for vitamin A for the adult male and female 10 years of age and older is the same.
    B. The Recommended Daily Allowance for vitamin A is expressed in terms of U.S.P. units.
    C. Vegetables have vitamin A activity equal to vitamin A in animal foods.
    D. Excessive amounts of vitamin A are well tolerated by adults.

8. Iron is a mineral required for growth and to keep the body functioning properly. Of the following, the combination of foods that will provide the BEST intake of iron is 8.____

    A. green peas, liver, enriched bread, dried potatoes
    B. cheese, oranges, liver, butter

C. peanut butter, milk, carrots, liver
D. liver, ice cream, chicken, peaches

9. Calcium and phosphorous account for approximately three-fourths of the mineral elements in the body. Their intake is important for adequate nutrition.
Which one of the following statements is CORRECT about both minerals?

   A. For children and young adults, the Recommended Daily Allowance for calcium is twice that for phosphorous.
   B. Their absorption and utilization are enhanced by the presence of vitamin E.
   C. They are not found in soft tissues.
   D. They constitute an important buffer system in the regulation of body neutrality.

10. When a menu is being planned for a specific holiday, the one of the following which is LEAST appropriate is to

    A. ask for suitable menu possibilities from the staff
    B. choose only foods which are familiar to those who will be served
    C. test acceptability of possible holiday items by serving one or two items at earlier meals
    D. include traditional foods associated with the holiday, if available

11. When a No. 8 scoop is used to serve mashed potatoes, the portion served should be _____ cup.

    A. 2/5   B. 1/3   C. 1/2   D. 2/3

12. A six-ounce ladle is equal to APPROXIMATELY _____ cup(s).

    A. 1/2   B. 1   C. 3/4   D. 1 1/4

13. The MOST accurate measurement of food is by

    A. volume
    B. weight
    C. can size
    D. number of pieces per container

14. Deep fat frying is BEST accomplished at which one of the following temperatures?

    A. 300° F   B. 350° F   C. 400° F   D. 450° F

15. When you are roasting beef, the indication that a well-done and palatable product has been achieved is an interior temperature in the range of

    A. 110° to 130° F   B. 131° to 150° F
    C. 151° to 170° F   D. 171° to 190° F

16. Of the following methods of roasting beef, the one that causes the LEAST amount of shrinkage is cooking at

    A. high temperature during the first half of the cooking time and at low temperature during the other half
    B. high temperature during the entire cooking time

C. moderate temperature during the first half of the cooking time and at high temperature during the other half
D. low temperature during the entire cooking time

17. The method of meat preparation that calls for cutting the meat into small pieces, covering with hot liquid, and cooking at about 185° F is known as   17._____

   A. boiling   B. stewing   C. roasting   D. broiling

18. Of the following pressure ranges, the one in which three compartment steamers operate is the _____ lb. range.   18._____

   A. 1-5   B. 5-15   C. 15-30   D. 30-50

19. When vegetables are cooked for large numbers of people, the BEST results are obtained by *batch cooking*.   19._____
   This kind of cooking is done in order to

   A. have high-quality vegetables available during the entire serving period
   B. prepare more vegetables using less staff
   C. use less equipment
   D. prepare several batches of vegetables at the same time

20. The one of the following procedures that could cause food poisoning is   20._____

   A. allowing cooked poultry to stand for an hour, slicing it, and covering it with broth, and holding it at room temperature for several hours
   B. keeping food mixtures on cafeteria counters for one hour
   C. cooking left-over food mixtures quickly by frequent stirring and then refrigerating in shallow pans
   D. chilling all ingredients for salads for at least one hour before preparation

21. When large numbers of people are to be served in a cafeteria setting, an estimate should be made each day of the quantity of food to be prepared and cooked.   21._____
   This is BEST done by which one of the following ways?

   A. Having the cook make a list of the previous day's leftovers.
   B. Considering previous sales of the same menu combinations, as well as the weather and any special events.
   C. Cooking as much food as the staff and equipment allow so as not to be caught short.
   D. Using the capacity of the seating area as a base.

22. Which one of the following statements concerning frozen pre-cooked foods is NOT correct?   22._____

   A. Certain pre-cooked foods are excellent when freshly prepared, but deteriorate rapidly in an ordinary freezer.
   B. Some pre-cooked foods are so greatly changed by freezing and subsequent reheating that they become unpalatable.
   C. All food items which are carefully cooked, rapidly frozen, and then held at low temperature until used, are satisfactory products when served.
   D. Many foods may be frozen, stored in an appropriate type of freezer, and thawed without marked change in nutritional and esthetic value.

23. Of the following, the one which is NOT a method of controlling food costs in an institutional food service is

   A. avoiding the use of *leftover* foods since they are usually unpopular items
   B. maintaining an accurate food inventory
   C. knowing what yield can be obtained from various sizes, counts, and amounts of food
   D. ensuring the food-service employees use standardized recipes and portions

24. The direct labor cost involved in the preparation of meals includes wages paid to cooks, bakers, salad makers, counter workers, etc. and is MOST accurately determined by which one of the following methods?

   A. Making studies of the amount of time spent by employees in actual meal preparation tasks.
   B. Checking employees' time cards to determine total absence time.
   C. Dividing the number of meals served each week by the number of employees.
   D. Determining how much time is lost because of equipment breakdown and adding the value of this time to the cost of employees' wages.

25. Which one of the following would MOST likely enable the supervisor of a food service to attain better cost control over operations?

   A. *Increasing* the output of individual staff members.
   B. *Increasing* the size of the staff.
   C. *Reducing* the amount of time scheduled for food preparation tasks.
   D. *Reducing* the amount of time spent on training staff members.

KEY (CORRECT ANSWERS)

1. D		11. C	
2. C		12. C	
3. B		13. B	
4. B		14. B	
5. A		15. D	
6. A		16. D	
7. A		17. B	
8. A		18. B	
9. D		19. A	
10. B		20. A	

21. B
22. C
23. A
24. A
25. A

TEST 2

DIRECTIONS: Each question or incomplete statement is followed by several suggested answers or completions. Select the one that BEST answers the question or completes the statement. *PRINT THE LETTER OF THE CORRECT ANSWER IN THE SPACE AT THE RIGHT.*

1. Of the following, the FIRST step in the control of food costs in an institution should be to   1.____

    A. make sure the delivery of foods is in accordance with the order
    B. store foods under tight security as soon as they are received
    C. follow purchase specifications in obtaining food products
    D. get the correct amount of raw food to the cook

2. Of the following, the area in which recipe costing aids are of MOST value is   2.____

    A. making yield studies
    B. planning menus
    C. taking inventories
    D. determining the cost of wasted foods

3. Control records of both the physical and cost aspects of food storage are MOST useful as a basic guide in which one of the following areas?   3.____

    A. Receiving food deliveries
    B. Issuing food to the kitchen
    C. Ordering food
    D. Controlling food theft

4. The one of the following which indicates actual control over food costs in a food service is that   4.____

    A. recipe costing is done
    B. waste is eliminated
    C. yield studies are made
    D. food cost data are regularly analyzed

5. The one of the following which is the MAJOR purpose of a perpetual inventory in the food storage area of a kitchen or other dietary unit is to   5.____

    A. facilitate removal of shelf items that are needed for quick use
    B. reduce breakage and spoilage of liquified foods
    C. act as a control in the area of food purchasing
    D. facilitate the planning of balanced diets and menus

6. Walk-in storage refrigerators can be a very important aspect of a well-equipped kitchen in a food service.   6.____
    Of the following, the MOST desirable location for a walk-in refrigerator is near the

    A. receiving and preparation areas
    B. tray delivery area
    C. cafeteria
    D. dishwashing area

7. Food specifications are precise statements of quality and other commodity requirements. All food should be purchased according to specifications.
Of the following, the LEAST important aspect of a food specification is the

   A. quantity required in a case, pound, carton, etc.
   B. federal grade desired
   C. size of the container
   D. picture of the item

8. The aim in buying food is to obtain the best value for the money spent.
Of the following, the practice which is LEAST likely to accomplish that aim is

   A. buying the cheapest item
   B. purchasing by specification
   C. purchasing only the quantities required for the menus planned
   D. checking all purchases on delivery

9. When deciding whether to select a particular piece of equipment for a kitchen or other dietary area, the one of the following which would be LEAST important for you to take into consideration is

   A. whether there is space for it
   B. whether it is easily cleaned and maintained
   C. whether there is an employee currently on staff who knows how to operate it
   D. how well it has worked in other institutions

10. Of the following foods, the type that is MOST likely to cause staph food poisoning if improperly prepared or handled is _____ food.

    A. sugar-coated   B. dried
    C. pickled   D. cream-filled

11. Harmful bacteria are MOST often introduced into foods prepared in a food service operation by

    A. insects   B. rodents   C. employees   D. utensils

12. When planning menus for secondary school students, it is desirable for the manager to do all of the following EXCEPT to

    A. stay within the school's food budget
    B. include familiar ethnic foods
    C. include many food choices
    D. consider the size of the food service staff

13. Of the following, the manager's BEST evidence for a shortage claim on surplus food delivered to a school is

    A. her written report of the shortage claim
    B. the delivery receipt from the truck driver
    C. the container the food was delivered in
    D. an old container of the same item

14. The manager should prepare school lunch menus for a MINIMUM of _____ week(s) at a time.   14._____

    A. one B. two C. three D. four

15. The manager must keep monthly inventories of all of the following EXCEPT   15._____

    A. paper goods B. food items
    C. serving utensils D. cleaning supplies

16. In the Type A lunch pattern for 10- to 12-year-old children, all of the following fulfill the *meat or meat alternate* requirement EXCEPT   16._____

    A. two ounces of cheese
    B. one-half cup of fresh carrots
    C. four tablespoons of peanut butter
    D. one-half cup of cooked dry peas

17. A manager is planning to use tuna fish salad to comply with the guideline for the *meat or meat alternate* requirement of the Type A lunch for secondary school students. How much tuna fish will she need in order to serve 400 secondary school students? _____ pounds.   17._____

    A. $37\frac{1}{2}$ B. 50 C. 75 D. 100

Questions 18-25.

DIRECTIONS: Answer Questions 18 through 25 SOLELY on the basis of information presented in the charts below.

STUDENT SALES COUNTER SHEET
March 4, 2005

Item	Price per Item	No. Items Offered for Sale	No. Items Unsold	Total Cash Received for Items Sold
Hot lunch	$2.25	250	75	
Milk	$0.60	525		$285.00
Soda	$0.75	300	163	$102.75
Ice Cream Bars	$0.45	181	59	$54.90
Buttered Roll	$0.15	200	150	
Cooked Vegetable	$0.90	325	40	$256.50
Pudding	$0.45	565	30	$240.75
Potato Chips	$0.30	610	50	$168.00

STUDENT SALES COUNTER SHEET
March 5, 2005

Item	Price per Item	No. Items Offered for Sale	No. Items Unsold	Total Cash Received for Items Sold
Hot lunch	$2.25	300		$585.00
Milk	$0.60	450		$255.00
Soda	$0.75	275	207	
Ice Cream Bars	$0.45	250	100	
Buttered Roll	$0.15	175	25	
Cooked Vegetable	$0.90	300	62	$214.20
Pudding	$0.45	490	47	
Potato Chips	$0.30	595	45	

18. Hot lunches accounted for APPROXIMATELY what percentage of all cash received for March 4, 2005?

    A. 10%   B. 15%   C. 20%   D. 25%

19. Which one of the following items was sold LEAST on March 4, 2005 and March 5, 2005, combined?

    A. Soda   B. Ice cream bars
    C. Buttered roll D. Cooked vegetable

20. The number of milk containers which were unsold on March 4, 2005 is

    A. 30   B. 50   C. 75   D. 95

21. How many fewer containers of pudding and soda were sold on March 5, 2005 than were sold on March 4, 2005?

    A. 19   B. 81   C. 105   D. 161

22. Which single item, besides hot lunches, accounted for the GREATEST number of items sold on March 4, 2005?

    A. Cooked vegetable   B. Pudding
    C. Ice cream bars   D. Soda

23. How many hot lunches were sold on March 4, 2005 and March 5, 2005, combined?

    A. 435   B. 550   C. 625   D. 665

24. Of the following, the item that was bought MOST by the students on both March 4, 2005 and March 5, 2005 is

    A. soda   B. buttered roll
    C. pudding   D. potato chips

25. The cumulative total of money received for all the soda, ice cream bars, buttered rolls, and pudding sold on March 4, 2005 is

    A. $165.15   B. $405.90   C. $858.90   D. $1252.65

KEY (CORRECT ANSWERS)

1.	C	11.	C
2.	B	12.	C
3.	C	13.	C
4.	B	14.	D
5.	C	15.	C
6.	A	16.	B
7.	D	17.	C
8.	A	18.	D
9.	C	19.	C
10.	D	20.	B

21. D
22. B
23. A
24. D
25. B

EXAMINATION SECTION
TEST 1

DIRECTIONS: Each question or incomplete statement is followed by several suggested answers or completions. Select the one that BEST answers the question or completes the statement. *PRINT THE LETTER OF THE CORRECT ANSWER IN THE SPACE AT THE RIGHT.*

1. Senna is obtained from 1.____

   A. cassia
   B. red peppers
   C. camomile
   D. tannin

2. Tapioca is made from a 2.____

   A. seed pod
   B. pomegranate
   C. melon
   D. shrub root stock

3. Tapioca flour is used for all of the following purposes EXCEPT 3.____

   A. tapioca
   B. postage stamp adhesive
   C. cotton fabric finishing
   D. synthetic fabric coloring

4. A blend of ground spices having no established formula is called 4.____

   A. curry powder
   B. all-spice
   C. poultry seasoning
   D. mixed spices

5. When onions are dried and ground, they are called 5.____

   A. onion salt
   B. oregano
   C. garlic
   D. onion powder

6. Allspice is derived from 6.____

   A. the berry of the pimento tree
   B. a mixture of nutmeg, cinnamon, and cloves
   C. the root of the allspice tree
   D. the bark of the cassia tree

7. Soy sauce is made from soybeans and 7.____

   A. lotus root
   B. brine and wheat
   C. rice
   D. mushrooms

8. Tapioca is prepared 8.____

   A. by hydrolyzing fructose
   B. by hydrolyzing starch
   C. from the root of the cassava
   D. from the root of the glycerriza

9. In dressings, an example of a *permanent emulsion* is 9.____

   A. french dressing
   B. mineral oil
   C. mayonnaise dressing
   D. olive oil

10. Of the following, the MOST inexpensive source of nutritive food is

   A. soybean   B. cereal   C. eggs   D. meats

11. When making medium white sauce, the ratio of fat to flour per cup of milk is

   A. 1 tsp to 1 tsp
   B. 2 Tbsp to 2 Tbsp
   C. 1 Tbsp to 1 Tbsp
   D. 1 Tbsp to 2 Tbsp

12. Of the following list of vegetables, all are economical to use EXCEPT

   A. dried legumes
   B. kale
   C. cabbage
   D. romaine

13. To store salad greens in the refrigerator, wash them and

   A. place on a china plate
   B. place in an air-tight container
   C. wrap in a brown paper bag
   D. wrap in a plastic bag with air holes

14. Root vegetables are BEST stored in atmosphere that is maintained

   A. at 36° F
   B. dehumidified
   C. at 30° F
   D. at 75% humidity

15. Before cooking, the vegetable that MUST be soaked in water is

   A. string beans
   B. brussels sprouts
   C. turnips
   D. celery

16. Deterioration of dried vegetables is retarded by

   A. marinating before drying
   B. storage in metal boxes
   C. precooking before drying
   D. infrared light treatment before packaging

17. The fibrous material in fruit and vegetables is

   A. connective tissue
   B. pith
   C. cellulose
   D. mineral matter

18. Green vegetables should be

   A. cooked in large amount of boiling salted water uncovered
   B. cooked covered in small amount of boiling water and served at once
   C. started in cold water and brought quickly to boil covered
   D. cooked in small amount of water with addition of soda

19. Spinach should be cooked

   A. in boiling water, without a cover
   B. dry, in an open pot
   C. dry, in a covered pot
   D. in boiling water, with a cover

20. Artichokes are scarce because they   20._____

    A. are in slight demand
    B. are difficult to digest
    C. do not keep well
    D. require special cultivation

21. Tea that has been dried after partial oxidation of the leaves is called   21._____

    A. green
    B. black
    C. oolong
    D. smoky souchong

22. The purpose of roasting coffee beans is to   22._____

    A. prevent mold growth
    B. prevent fermentation
    C. develop flavor
    D. drive out moisture

23. Coffee is NOT recommended for children because it   23._____

    A. is too strong for children
    B. does not contain any nutrients and has caffeine
    C. will keep children awake at night
    D. is too expensive

24. In comparison with regular cocoa, instant cocoa is   24._____

    A. more nutritious
    B. less digestible
    C. less costly
    D. more costly

25. Legumes and nuts provide a rich source of   25._____

    A. thiamine   B. calcium   C. niacin   D. sodium

KEY (CORRECT ANSWERS)

1. A		11. B	
2. D		12. D	
3. D		13. D	
4. A		14. A	
5. D		15. B	
6. A		16. C	
7. C		17. C	
8. C		18. B	
9. C		19. D	
10. A		20. D	

21. C
22. C
23. B
24. D
25. A

TEST 2

DIRECTIONS: Each question or incomplete statement is followed by several suggested answers or completions. Select the one that BEST answers the question or completes the statement. *PRINT THE LETTER OF THE CORRECT ANSWER IN THE SPACE AT THE RIGHT.*

1. Rocky Mountain spotted fever in cattle is spread by

    A. mosquitoes
    B. sewage disposal in rivers
    C. animal ticks
    D. rodents in granaries

2. Frozen meat is BEST preserved when stored

    A. in cheesecloth at 20° F
    B. unwrapped at 0° F
    C. in moisture-proof material at 0° F
    D. unwrapped at -20° F

3. The MOST tender cuts of beef are from the

    A. loin and rib
    B. leg and rib
    C. shoulder and loin
    D. rump and neck

4. The government stamp on meats indicates

    A. date when slaughtered
    B. point of origin
    C. nutritional value
    D. quality

5. An effective method for tenderizing meats that are tough is

    A. braising   B. broiling   C. frying   D. roasting

6. Chuck steak should be

    A. pan-fried   B. broiled   C. roasted   D. baked

7. Meat should be stored in the refrigerator overnight for use on the next day

    A. loosely covered with patapar in the freezing unit
    B. tightly covered with aluminum foil in a cool part
    C. covered with aluminum foil in the freezing unit
    D. loosely covered with wax paper in a cool part

8. As to pork, the federal meat inspection law should be amended to require examination for

    A. botulism   B. trichina   C. tetanus   D. fastigium

9. To retard spoilage of bread, baking companies may add sodium

    A. benzoate
    B. propionate
    C. sulphationate
    D. hypophosphate

2 (#2)

10. The freshness of an egg is recognized by the 10._____

    A. thinness of the shell
    B. light color of the yolk
    C. absence of blood spots
    D. size of the air cell

11. When buying eggs, it is important to remember that the food value 11._____

    A. of grade A eggs is greater than that of grade C eggs
    B. is governed by the color of the egg shell
    C. is not affected by blood spots
    D. depends on the grade of eggs

12. Egg whites beat BEST if they are 12._____

    A. warm   B. chilled thoroughly
    C. at room temperature   D. beaten by hand

13. The critical temperatures for eggs in storage are 13._____

    A. 28° and 68°   B. 32° and 75°
    C. 38° and 60°   D. 25° and 75°

14. Soft dough is used for 14._____

    A. pie   B. biscuits (baking powder)
    C. cake (butter)   D. muffins

15. One pound of dried eggs is equivalent to _____ eggs. 15._____

    A. 50-60   B. 30-40   C. 20-25   D. 15-18

16. To store eggs at home, 16._____

    A. keep them exposed on the cupboard
    B. wash and place them in the refrigerator
    C. do not wash, and place them in the refrigerator
    D. place them in a moderately cool place

17. Eggs stored in the home should be 17._____

    A. uncovered in the refrigerator
    B. washed
    C. in a cool place but not in the refrigerator
    D. in a refrigerator in a covered container

18. Yeast 18._____

    A. is usually present in the air
    B. flourishes at temperatures above 150° F
    C. requires carbon dioxide for optimum development
    D. multiplies rapidly in bright sunlight

19. Yeasts and molds are destroyed by

   A. high temperature in the pressure cooker
   B. one hour exposure to sub-zero temperature (F.)
   C. exposing the cardboard container to infrared light
   D. decreasing the moisture content of the food on which they rest

20. Carbon dioxide is a final product of yeast fermentation because of which of the following enzymes?

   A. Zymase   B. Diastase   C. Protease   D. Maltase

21. *Precooking* of dry cereals

   A. softens the cellulose
   B. prevents molding
   C. renders the cellulose digestible
   D. insures a smooth product when cooked

22. Yeast plants grow BEST at the Fahrenheit temperature of

   A. 70-75°   B. 80-85°   C. 90-95°   D. 100-105°

23. The number of tablespoonfuls of lemon juice to be added to each cup of sweet milk for a sour milk recipe is

   A. 1/2   B. 1   C. 1 1/2   D. 2

24. Baking powder consists of

   A. baking soda, an acid salt, and a starch
   B. iron, carbon dioxide, and fat
   C. baking soda, salt, and starch
   D. carbohydrate, protein, and fat

25. When sugar is used in cooking,

   A. acids soften cellulose
   B. alkalies invert sugar
   C. acids invert sugar
   D. dry heat changes sucrose to glucose

KEY (CORRECT ANSWERS)

1. C
2. C
3. A
4. D
5. A

6. D
7. C
8. B
9. B
10. D

11. C
12. C
13. A
14. B
15. B

16. C
17. D
18. A
19. A
20. B

21. A
22. B
23. C
24. A
25. C

TEST 3

DIRECTIONS: Each question or incomplete statement is followed by several suggested answers or completions. Select the one that BEST answers the question or completes the statement. *PRINT THE LETTER OF THE CORRECT ANSWER IN THE SPACE AT THE RIGHT.*

1. Milk is heated in a double boiler to prevent

    A. curdling
    B. burning
    C. coagulation of the protein
    D. dehomogenization

    1.____

2. Yeast plants grow BEST at a temperature of _____ °F.

    A. 70-75   B. 80-85   C. 90-95   D. 100-105

    2.____

3. The kind of meat that may safely be stored LONGEST after freezing is

    A. lamb   B. veal   C. pork   D. beef

    3.____

4. Federal inspection is required for all meat sold

    A. in cities of a population of 50,000 and over
    B. under a brand name
    C. in interstate commerce
    D. anywhere in the United States

    4.____

5. At home, frozen meats should be kept at a temperature of

    A. 0° F   B. 15° F   C. 32° F   D. 45° F

    5.____

6. Leftover meat can be wrapped and frozen, but should be used before

    A. 1 week   B. 1 month   C. 3 months   D. 6 months

    6.____

7. Meat which is well-marbled is classified as

    A. good   B. utility
    C. pre-cooked   D. choice

    7.____

8. After being dressed, a chicked should be cooked not later than _____ hours.

    A. 6   B. 24   C. 48   D. 96

    8.____

9. The number of times brown rice will increase in volume while cooking is

    A. 0   B. 2   C. 4   D. 6

    9.____

10. The color of the Federal United States *Inspected and Passed* stamp on meat is

    A. red   B. blue   C. brown   D. purple

    10.____

11. Yeasts and molds are destroyed by

    A. decreasing the moisture content of the foods in which they rest
    B. one hour exposure to sub-zero F.

    11.____

46

C. exposure of the container to infrared light
D. high temperature in a pressure cooker

12. The MOST nourishing part of the cereal grain is the

    A. bran
    B. aleurone layer
    C. germ
    D. endosperm

13. Of the following, the cereal which is comparatively rich in fats is

    A. rye   B. wheat   C. rice   D. oats

14. The advantage of using a whole-grain cereal is that it

    A. has a distinctive flavor
    B. cooks quickly
    C. contains vitamins and minerals
    D. looks attractive

15. Macaroni is made from a kind of wheat called

    A. endosperm   B. durum   C. gluten   D. duroc

16. The advantage of a hot cereal over a dry cereal is that it

    A. gives more warmth to the body
    B. contains more minerals and vitamins
    C. helps you to gain weight
    D. costs less

17. When buying cereal, to check a boxed package for infestation by weevils, one should

    A. look for the inspection seal
    B. check the corners for tiny holes
    C. request the store manager to inspect the box
    D. check the integrity of the processor

18. The LARGEST percentage of gluten is found in flour made from

    A. rye   B. barley   C. oats   D. wheat

19. The freshness of an egg is recognizable by

    A. the size of the air cell
    B. absence of blood spots
    C. light color of the yolk
    D. the thickness of the shell

20. Molasses is rich in

    A. potassium   B. iron   C. vitamin C   D. niacin

21. Over the last hundred years, the per capital consumption of sugar in the United States has INCREASED _____ percent.

    A. 900   B. 150   C. 500   D. 300

22. Among the following, the salt-water fish is

    A. perch   B. pickerel   C. mackerel   D. muskalonge

23. Fish just as it is taken from the water is called

    A. fillet fish   B. lutfish
    C. round fish   D. freshwater fish

24. Shellfish with segmented shells are called

    A. crustaceans   B. mollusks
    C. clams   D. mussels

25. *Green Shrimp* are shrimp which are

    A. uncooked   B. too small for eating
    C. too young for harvesting   D. giant size

KEY (CORRECT ANSWERS)

1.	B	11.	A
2.	D	12.	D
3.	D	13.	D
4.	C	14.	C
5.	A	15.	B
6.	C	16.	D
7.	D	17.	B
8.	C	18.	D
9.	C	19.	A
10.	D	20.	B

21. D
22. C
23. C
24. A
25. A

READING COMPREHENSION
UNDERSTANDING AND INTERPRETING WRITTEN MATERIAL
EXAMINATION SECTION
TEST 1

DIRECTIONS: Each question or incomplete statement is followed by several suggested answers or completions. Select the one that BEST answers the question or completes the statement. *PRINT THE LETTER OF THE CORRECT ANSWER IN THE SPACE AT THE RIGHT.*

Questions 1-4.

DIRECTIONS: Questions 1 through 4 are to be answered SOLELY on the basis of the following paragraph.

Rodent control must be planned carefully in order to insure its success. This means that more knowledge is needed about the habits and favorite breeding places of Domestic Rats than any other kind. A favorite breeding place for Domestic Rats is known to be in old or badly constructed buildings. Rats find these buildings very comfortable for making nests. However, the only way to gain this kind of detailed knowledge about rats is through careful study.

1. According to the above paragraph, rats find comfortable nesting places 1.____

    A. in old buildings   B. in pipes
    C. on roofs   D. in sewers

2. The paragraph states that the BEST way to learn all about the favorite nesting places of rats is by 2.____

    A. asking people   B. careful study
    C. using traps   D. watching ratholes

3. According to the paragraph, in order to insure the success of rodent control, it is necessary to 3.____

    A. design better bait   B. give out more information
    C. plan carefully   D. use pesticides

4. The paragraph states that the MOST important rats to study are _____ Rats. 4.____

    A. African   B. Asian   C. Domestic   D. European

Questions 5-8.

DIRECTIONS: Questions 5 through 8 are to be answered SOLELY on the basis of the following paragraph.

People are very suspicious of all strangers who knock at their door. For this reason, every pest control aide, whether man or woman, must carry an identification card at all times on the job. These cards are issued by the agency the aide works for. The aide's picture is on the card. The aide's name is typed in, and the aide's signature is written on the line below.

49

The name, address, and telephone number of the agency issuing the card is also printed on it. Once the aide shows this ID card to prove his or her identity, the tenant's time should not be taken up with small talk. The tenant should be told briefly what pest control means. The aide should be polite and ready to answer any questions the tenant may have on the subject. Then, the aide should thank the tenant for listening and say goodbye.

5. According to the above paragraph, when she visits tenants, the one item a pest control aide must ALWAYS carry with her is a(n)

    A. badge
    B. driver's license
    C. identification card
    D. watch

6. According to the paragraph, a pest control aide is supposed to talk to each tenant he visits

    A. at length about the agency
    B. briefly about pest control
    C. at length about family matters
    D. briefly about social security

7. According to the paragraph, the item that does NOT appear on an ID card is the

    A. address of the agency
    B. name of the agency
    C. signature of the aide
    D. social security number of the aide

8. According to the paragraph, a pest control aide carries an identification card because he must

    A. prove to tenants who he is
    B. provide the tenant with the agency's address
    C. provide the tenant with the agency's telephone number
    D. save the tenant's time

Questions 9-12.

DIRECTIONS: Questions 9 through 12 are to be answered SOLELY on the basis of the following paragraphs.

The insects you, as a Housing Exterminator, will control are just a minute fraction of the millions which inhabit the world. Man does well to hold his own in the face of the constant pressures that insects continue to exert upon him. Not only are the total numbers tremendous, but the number of individual kinds, or species, certainly exceeds 800,000 — a number greater than that of all other animals combined. Many of these are beneficial, but some are especially competitive with man. Not only are insects numerous, but they are among the most adaptable of all animals. In their many forms, they are fitted for almost any specific way of life. Their adaptability, combined with their tremendous rate of reproduction, gives insects an unequaled potential for survival

The food of insects includes almost anything that can be eaten by any other animal, as well as many things which cannot even be digested by any other animals. Most insects do not harm the products of man or carry diseases harmful to him; however, many do carry diseases, and others feed on his food and manufactured goods. Some are adapted to living only in open areas, while others are able to live in extremely confined spaces. All of these factors combined make the insects a group of animals having many members which are a nuisance to man and thus of great importance to the Housing Exterminator.

The control of insects requires an understanding of their way of life. Thus, it is necessary for the Housing Exterminator to understand the anatomy of the insect, its method of growth, the time it takes for the insect to grow from egg to adult, its habits, the stage of its life history in which it causes damage, its food, and its common living places. In order to obtain the best control, it is especially important to be able to identify correctly the specific insect involved because without this knowledge, it is impossible to prescribe a proper treatment.

9. Which one of the following is a CORRECT statement about the insect population of the world according to the above paragraph?
The

   A. total number of insects is less than the total number of all other animals combined
   B. number of species of insects is greater than the number of species of all other animals combined
   C. total number of harmful insects is greater than the total number of those which are not harmful
   D. number of species of harmless insects is less than the number of species of those which are harmful

10. Insects will be controlled MOST efficiently if the Housing Exterminator

   A. understands why the insects are so numerous
   B. knows what insects he is dealing with
   C. sees if the insects compete with man
   D. is able to identify the food which the insects digest

11. According to the above passage, insects are of importance to an exterminator PRIMARILY because they

   A. can be annoying, destructive, and harmful to man
   B. are able to thrive in very small spaces
   C. cause damage during their growth stages
   D. are so adaptable that they can adjust to any environment

12. According to the above passage, insects can eat

   A. everything that any other living thing can eat
   B. man's food and things which he makes
   C. anything which other animals can't digest
   D. only food and food products

Questions 13-22.

DIRECTIONS: Questions 13 through 22 are to be answered SOLELY on the basis of the following instructions.

INSTRUCTIONS FOR PREPARATION AND PLACEMENT OF RAT BAITS

1. Fresh baits are the most acceptable to rats, so mix only enough bait for current needs. Use a binder of molasses or of vegetable, mineral or fish oil in cereal or dry baits to hold the poison and the dry bait together and to aid in mixing.

2. Mix an emetic, usually tartar emetic, with zinc phosphide and other more toxic bait formulations to protect animals other than rodents, even though acceptability of such baits to the rodents is thereby reduced.

3. Mix bait as directed. Too much poison may give the bait a strong taste or odor. Too little will not kill but may result in bait shyness. Excessive amounts of poison increase the danger to man and to domestic animals.

4. Mix baits well. Poor mixing results in non-uniform baits and poor kills and speeds development of *bait shyness*. Mechanical bait-mixing equipment is necessary where large quantities of bait are mixed routinely.

5. Clearly label poisons and mixing equipment. Do not use bait-mixing equipment for other purposes. Lock up poisons and mixing equipment when not in use. Treat all poisons with respect. Read and follow all label instructions. Avoid inhaling powders or getting poisons on hands, clothes, or utensils from which they may reach the mouth. Wear rubber gloves when handling poisons. Always mix poisons in a well-ventilated place, particularly when mixing dry ingredients.

6. If anticoagulant baits are used, they should be placed in paper, metal, or plastic pie plates or in permanent bait stations. Be liberal in baiting. For anticoagulants to be fully effective, repeated doses must be consumed by every rodent at a given location for a period of five or more consecutive days.

7. Protect animals other than domestic rodents, and shield baits from the weather under shelter or with bait boxes, boards, pipes, or cans.

8. Note locations of all bait containers so that inspections can be made rapidly and the bait that has been consumed can be quickly replaced. (Bait consumption is generally heavy right after initial placement, making daily inspection and replacement advisable for the first 3 days after regular feeding begins.)

9. At each inspection, smooth the surface of the baits so that new signs of feeding will show readily. Replace moldy, wet, caked, or insect-infested baits with fresh ones. If a bait remains undisturbed for several successive inspections, move it to an area showing fresh rodent signs.

10. Use shallow bait containers fastened to the floor or containers of sufficient weight to prevent the rodents from overturning them or dragging them to their burrows. A roofing tack driven through metal or fiber containers into the floor reduces spillage.

11. When single-dose poisons are used, wrap one-shot poison food baits in 4" x 4" paper squares to form torpedoes about the size of a large olive. These may be tossed readily into otherwise inaccessible places. If several types of bait such as meat, fish, or cereal are to be distributed at the same time, a different color of paper should be used for each of the various types of bait.

12. Be generous with baits. Too few baits, or poorly placed baits, may miss many rodents. Bait liberally where signs of rat activity are numerous and recent. In light or moderate infestations, torpedoes containing a single-dose poison, such as red squill, have given good control when applied at a minimum rate of 20 baits per private residence. As many as 100 to 200 baits may be required for premises with heavy rodent infestations.

13. Place baits in hidden sites out of reach of children and pets.

14. Inspect and rebait as needed, using another poison and another bait material when the rats become shy of the original baits.

13. According to the above instructions, if you find, upon inspection, that your baits are overrun with insects, you SHOULD

    A. replace the baits with fresh baits
    B. move the baits to another station
    C. add more rodenticide to the baits and re-mix them
    D. apply the appropriate insecticide to the baits

14. According to the above instructions, if an exterminator wants to make sure he does NOT get poor kills, he SHOULD

    A. mix large quantities of baits routinely
    B. stick to one poison
    C. mix the baits well
    D. use deep bait containers that cannot be easily overturned

15. According to the above instructions, the equipment which is used for mixing bait should be

    A. cleaned routinely
    B. mechanically easy to handle
    C. easily disposable
    D. labeled clearly

16. According to the above instructions, making the surface of the bait smooth every time that you inspect the bait containers is

    A. *proper* because it disturbs the insect infestation of the bait
    B. *improper* because it will make the bait even less uniform if it was already mixed poorly
    C. *proper* because it will help you determine if new signs of feeding are present
    D. *improper* because it increases the presence of human odor on the bait and discourages rodents

17. According to the above instructions, if you are making a bait with zinc phosphide, it is MOST important to

    A. prepare a generous amount so you can bait liberally where signs of rat activity are numerous
    B. use molasses to insure that the bait will be uniform
    C. shield the bait from the weather
    D. mix an emetic with the bait

18. According to the above instructions, you should substitute one poison for another poison when the

    A. bait consumption is heavy after initial placement
    B. rodents become shy of the original baits
    C. poison is dangerous to domestic animals
    D. rodents are able to drag the baits to their burrows

19. According to the above instructions, when you handle poisons, you SHOULD

   A. use mechanical bait-making equipment
   B. wear rubber gloves
   C. never place them in paper plates
   D. always mix them with moist ingredients

20. According to the above instructions, if you plan to distribute several types of bait at the same time in the form of *torpedoes*, you SHOULD

   A. select only anticoagulant baits for this purpose
   B. reduce the possibility of bait spillage by driving a roofing tack through the container into the floor
   C. use a different color of paper for each of the various types of bait
   D. make sure that the rodent does not consume repeated doses for more than a period of five consecutive days at the same location

21. According to the above instructions, mixing too much poison in the bait

   A. may bring about bait shyness
   B. permits the exterminator to make less frequent reinspections
   C. increases the danger to other life
   D. may be necessary when anticoagulants are used

22. According to the above instructions, if grain is to be used as bait,

   A. rodents will not accept it if it is mixed with fish oil
   B. the exterminator will only be able to make *torpedoes*
   C. it will not be necessary to check the bait for fresh rodent signs
   D. a binder should also be used to aid in mixing

Questions 23-25.

DIRECTIONS: Questions 23 through 25 are to be answered SOLELY on the basis of the following paragraphs.

The German roach is the most common roach in houses in the United States. Adults are pale brown and about 1/2-inch long; both sexes have wings as long as the body, and can be distinguished from other roaches by the two dark stripes on the pronotum. The female carries its egg capsule protruding from her abdomen until the eggs are ready to hatch. This is the only common house-infesting species which carries the egg capsule for such an extended period of time. A female will usually produce 4 to 8 capsules in her lifetime. Each capsule contains 30 to 48 eggs, which hatch out in about 28 days at ordinary room temperature. The completion of the nymphal stage under room conditions requires 40 to 125 days. German roaches may live as adults for as long as 303 days.

It is stated above that the German cockroach is the most commonly encountered of the house-infesting species in the United States. The reasons for this are somewhat complex, but the understanding of some of the factors involved are basic to the practice of pest control. In the first place, the German cockroach has a larger number of eggs per capsule and a shorter hatching time than do the other species. It also requires a shorter period from hatching until sexual maturity, so that within a given period of time, a population of German roaches will produce a larger number of eggs. On the basis of this fact, we can state that this species has a high reproductive potential. Since the female carries the egg capsule during nearly the entire time that the embryos are developing within the egg, many hazards of the environment which may affect the eggs are avoided. This means that more nymphs are likely to hatch and that a larger portion of the reproductive potential is realized. The nymphs which hatch from each egg capsule tend to stay close to each other; and since they are often close to the female at time of hatching, there is a tendency for the population density to be high locally. Being smaller than most of the other roaches, they are able to conceal themselves in many places which are inaccessible to individuals of the larger species. All of these factors combined help to give the German cockroach an advantage with regard to group survival.

23. According to the above passage, the MOST important feature of the German roach which gives it an advantage over other roaches is its

    A. distinctive markings
    B. immunity to disease
    C. long life span
    D. power to reproduce

24. An IMPORTANT difference between an adult female German roach and an adult female of other species is the

    A. black bars or stripes which appear on the abdomen of the German roach
    B. German roach's preference for warm, moist places in which to breed
    C. long period of time during which the German roach carries the egg capsule
    D. presence of longer wings on the female German roach

25. A storeroom in a certain housing project has an infestation of German roaches, which includes 125 adult females. If the infestation is not treated and ordinary room temperature is maintained in the storeroom, how many eggs will hatch out during the lifetime of these females if they each lay 8 capsules containing 48 eggs each?

    A. 1,500   B. 48,000   C. 96,000   D. 303,000

KEY (CORRECT ANSWERS)

1. A
2. B
3. C
4. C
5. C

6. B
7. D
8. A
9. B
10. B

11. A
12. B
13. A
14. C
15. D

16. C
17. D
18. B
19. B
20. C

21. C
22. D
23. D
24. C
25. B

TEST 2

DIRECTIONS: Each question or incomplete statement is followed by several suggested answers or completions. Select the one that BEST answers the question or completes the statement. *PRINT THE LETTER OF THE CORRECT ANSWER IN THE SPACE AT THE RIGHT.*

Questions 1-10.

DIRECTIONS: Questions 1 through 10 are to be answered SOLELY on the basis of the information contained in the following passage and refer to entries that would be made on the Field Visit Report form that follows the passage.

On March 6, 2007, a crew composed of five Community Service Aides and three Pest Control Aides, under the supervision of a Crew Chief (Pest Control), made a field visit to inspect several residential buildings and a vacant lot. The purpose of the visit was to check for exposed refuse and signs of rats, mice, and insects. If conditions needed correction, they were to recommend the actions that should be taken.

The crew was driven in a department car to the first inspection site, an apartment house at 124 Grand Street, arriving at 11:30 A.M. When the crew members inspected the apartment house, they discovered rats and holes in the baseboards in several of the apartments. The landlord had not placed enough bait boxes in the basement. The Crew Chief recommended that an exterminator be scheduled to treat the building. The crew left the building at 12:05 P.M. and walked to the next inspection site at 129 Grand Street.

The crew arrived at the second site at 12:10 P.M. and left at 12:40 P.M. Because the crew found rats and roaches in the building, the Crew Chief immediately called the office and made arrangements for an exterminator to treat the building that afternoon. The Crew Chief recommended that the building should be re-inspected the following week to see if the exterminating had been successful.

The crew workers walked to the next inspection site, a vacant lot on Lucke Street, across the street from an apartment building at 350 Lucke Street. They observed that refuse covered much of the area of the vacant lot. The Crew Chief recommended that a clean-up team be scheduled to remove refuse from the lot.

The crew's last inspection of the day was a building at 300 Lucke Street. They walked to this site, arrived at 1:00 P.M., and stayed for an hour. They inspected several apartments in the building to see if a recent extermination had been successful. Upon seeing that no further work was needed at the site, they returned to their office by subway.

The Crew Chief arrived at the office at 3:00 P.M. and made out the following Field Visit Report form.

2 (#2)

FIELD VISIT REPORT FORM

1. Date_____
2. Time Arrived At First Site_____
3. Purpose of Field Visit_____
   _____
   _____
4. Number of Persons in Crew (Not including Crew Chief (Pest Control)_____
   _____
5. Transportation_____
6. Number of Sites Visited_____
7. Addresses of Sites Visited_____
   _____
   _____
   _____
8. Conditions Noted_____
   _____
   _____
   _____
9. Recommendations_____
   _____
   _____
   _____
10. Arrangements Made by Crew Chief While in the Field_____
    _____
    _____
    _____
11. Time Left Last Site_____

1. Which of the following should be entered on line 2?

   A. 11:30 A.M.   B. 12:05 P.M.
   C. 12:10 P.M.   D. 12:40 P.M.

2. Which of the following should be entered on line 3?

   A. Exterminate apartment buildings that have rats and mice
   B. Examine various sites for exposed refuse and signs of rats, mice, and Insects
   C. Inspect work done by clean-up team
   D. Clean up lots that are covered with refuse

3. The number that should be entered on line 4 is

   A. 3   B. 5   C. 8   D. 9

4. Which of the following should be entered on line 6?

   A. 3   B. 4   C. 5   D. 6

5. Each of the following should be entered on line 7 EXCEPT

   A. 124 Grand Street   B. 129 Grand Street
   C. 300 Lucke Street   D. 350 Lucke Street

6. Each of the following should be entered on line 8 EXCEPT the presence of

   A. holes in the baseboards at 124 Grand Street
   B. insects, rats, and mice at 300 Lucke Street
   C. refuse at the vacant lot on Lucke Street
   D. rats and roaches at 129 Grand Street

7. Which of the following should be entered on line 5? _____ between sites.

   A. Department car to first site, subway
   B. Subway to first site, walked
   C. Walked to first site, department car
   D. Department car to first site, walked

8. All of the following should be entered on line 9 EXCEPT

   A. extermination at 124 Grand Street to remove rats
   B. clean-up at the lot on Lucke Street to remove refuse
   C. follow-up visit at 129 Grand Street to determine success of extermination
   D. clean-up building at 300 Lucke Street to end infestation

9. Which of the following should be entered on line 10?

   A. Extermination of building at 129 Grand Street
   B. Extermination of building at 124 Grand Street
   C. Clean-up of lot on Lucke Street
   D. Clean-up of building at 300 Lucke Street

10. Which of the following should be entered on line 11?

    A. 12:40 P.M.
    B. 1:00 P.M.
    C. 2:00 P.M.
    D. 3:00 P.M.

Questions 11-14.

DIRECTIONS: Questions 11 through 14 are to be answered SOLELY on the basis of the following passage.

Sometimes an exterminator has to use a crowbar, for example, to open wooden crates that contain supplies which are shipped to the exterminating shop. He should know how to handle a crowbar so that he can use it safely. The danger involved in using a crowbar is that it may slip. A dull, broken crowbar is more likely to slip than one which has a sharp edge and a good *bite*. If the crowbar should slip or the object being opened should move suddenly, an exterminator's hand might be pinched or he might fall. The way in which he holds the crowbar and how he stands when using it can prevent such accidents. His hands should be dry when he uses a crowbar and, if he is wearing gloves, they should be free from grease. He should not work with the crowbar between his legs. When they are not being used, crowbars should be kept in a rack in the exterminating shop where they can not fall on someone or cause anyone to trip.

11. Of the following, the BEST title for the above passage is

    A. PROPER POSITION WHEN USING A CROWBAR
    B. TOOLS USED BY EXTERMINATORS
    C. USING A CROWBAR SAFELY
    D. WHEN TO USE A CROWBAR

12. A crowbar is MOST likely to slip if it

    A. has a good *bite*
    B. has a sharp edge
    C. is dull and broken
    D. is handled without gloves

13. Crowbars should be stored in a rack when they are not being used so that they will

    A. be easy to get at
    B. not cause accidents
    C. not be broken
    D. not be stolen

14. A worker should NOT use a crowbar if

    A. he is wearing gloves
    B. his hands are wet
    C. it has not been kept in a rack
    D. it has a sharp edge

Questions 15-17.

DIRECTIONS: Questions 15 through 17 are to be answered SOLELY on the basis of the following passage.

An exterminator should call the Fire Department for any fire except a small one in a wastebasket. This kind of fire can be put out with a fire extinguisher. If the exterminator is not sure about the size of the fire, he should not wait to find out how big it is. He should call the Fire Department at once.

Every exterminator should know what to do when a fire starts. He should know how to use the fire fighting tools in the building and how to call the Fire Department. He should also know where the nearest fire alarm box is. But the most important thing for an exterminator to do in case of fire is to avoid panic.

15. If there is a small fire in a wastebasket, an exterminator should

    A. call the Fire Department
    B. let it burn itself out
    C. open a window
    D. put it out with a fire extinguisher

16. In case of fire, the MOST important thing for an exterminator to do is to

    A. find out how big it is
    B. keep calm
    C. leave the building right away
    D. report to his boss

17. If a large fire starts while he is at work, an exterminator should always FIRST

    A. call the Fire Department
    B. notify the Housing Superintendent
    C. remove inflammables from the building
    D. use a fire extinguisher

Questions 18-19.

DIRECTIONS: Questions 18 and 19 are to be answered SOLELY on the basis of the following paragraph.

The cabinet shall be fabricated entirely of 22-gage stainless steel with #4 satin finish on all exposed surfaces. The face trim shall be one piece construction with no mitres or welding, 1" wide and 1/4" to the wall. All doors shall be mounted on heavy duty stainless steel piano hinges and have a concealed lock.

18. As used in the above paragraph, the word *fabricated* means MOST NEARLY   18.____

    A. made   B. designed   C. cut   D. plated

19. According to the above paragraph, a satin finish is to be used on surfaces   19.____

    A. to be welded
    B. that are visible
    C. on which the hinges are mounted
    D. that are to be covered

Questions 20-25.

DIRECTIONS: Questions 20 through 25 are to be answered SOLELY on the basis of the information contained in the following paragraph. Each question consists of a statement. You are to indicate whether the statement is TRUE (T) or FALSE (F).

CONTROL OF RABIES

The history of rabies in many countries proves the need for strong preventive measures. England is a good example. Rabies ran rampant in the British Isles during the American Revolution. In the 19th century, the country began to enforce strict measures: licensing all dogs, muzzling all dogs, and quarantining all incoming animals for 6 months' observation. An additional measure was the capturing and killing of all unlicensed *strays*.

As a result, rabies was completely eradicated, and similar measures have achieved the same results in Ireland, Denmark, Norway, Sweden, Australia, and Hawaii.

20. Rabies was prevalent in England about the year 1776.   20.____

21. By enforcement of strict measures in the 1800's, rabies was eliminated in England.   21.____

22. The only measures enforced in England for the control of rabies were the licensing and muzzling of all dogs.   22.____

23. Unlicensed dogs without owners were put to death when found.   23.____

24. A total of six countries, including England, obtained good results in combating rabies.   24.____

25. In three Scandinavian countries, rabies has been eliminated.   25.____

KEY (CORRECT ANSWERS)

1. A
2. B
3. C
4. B
5. D

6. B
7. D
8. D
9. A
10. C

11. C
12. C
13. B
14. B
15. D

16. B
17. A
18. A
19. B
20. T

21. T
22. F
23. T
24. F
25. T

ARITHMETICAL COMPUTATION AND REASONING
EXAMINATION SECTION
TEST 1

DIRECTIONS: Each question or incomplete statement is followed by several suggested answers or completions. Select the one that BEST answers the question or completes the statement. *PRINT THE LETTER OF THE CORRECT ANSWER IN THE SPACE AT THE RIGHT.*

1. 3/8 less than $40 is
   A. $25   B. $65   C. $15   D. $55   1._____

2. 27/64 expressed as a percent is
   A. 40.625%   B. 42.188%   C. 43.750%   D. 45.313%   2._____

3. 1/6 more than 36 gross is _____ gross.
   A. 6   B. 48   C. 30   D. 42   3._____

4. 15 is 20% of   4._____

5. The number which when increased by 1/3 of itself equals 96 is   5._____
   A. 128   B. 72   C. 64   D. 32

6. 0.16 3/4 written as percent is   6._____
   A. 16 3/4%   B. 16.3/4%   C. .016 3/4%   D. .0016 3/4%

7. 55% of 15 is   7._____
   A. 82.5   B. 0.825   C. 0.0825   D. 8.25

8. The number which when decreased by 1/3 of itself equals 96 is   8._____
   A. 64   B. 32   C. 128   D. 144

9. A carpenter used a board 15 3/4 ft. long from which 3 footstools were made with sufficient lumber left over for half of another footstool.   9._____
   If the lumber cost 24 1/2¢ per foot, the cost of EACH footstool was
   A. $1.54   B. $3.86   C. $1.10   D. $1.08

10. In one year, a luncheonette purchased 1231 gallons of milk for $907.99.   10._____
    The AVERAGE cost per half pint was
    A. $0.046   B. $0.045   C. $0.047   D. $0.044

11. The product of 23 and 9 3/4 is   11._____
    A. 191 2/3   B. 224 1/4   C. 213 3/4   D. 32 3/4

12. An order for 345 machine bolts at $4.15 per hundred will cost   12._____
    A. $0.1432   B. $1.1432   C. $14.32   D. $143.20

13. The fractional equivalent of .0625 is

    A. 1/16　　B. 1/15　　C. 1/14　　D. 1/13

14. The number 0.03125 equals

    A. 3/64　　B. 1/16　　C. 1/64　　D. 1/32

15. 21.70 divided by 1.75 equals

    A. 124　　B. 12.4　　C. 1.24　　D. .124

16. The average cost of school lunches for 100 children varied as follows: Monday, $0.285; Tuesday, $0.237; Wednesday, $0.264; Thursday, $0.276; Friday, $0.292. The AVERAGE lunch cost

    A. $0.136　　B. $0.270　　C. $0.135　　D. $0.271

17. The cost of 5 dozen eggs at $8.52 per gross is

    A. $3.50　　B. $42.60　　C. $3.55　　D. $3.74

18. 410.07 less 38.49 equals

    A. 372.58　　B. 371.58　　C. 381.58　　D. 382.68

19. The cost of 7 3/4 tons of coal at $20.16 per ton is

    A. $15.12　　B. $151.20　　C. $141.12　　D. $156.24

20. The sum of 90.79, 79.09, 97.90, and 9.97 is

    A. 277.75　　B. 278.56　　C. 276.94　　D. 277.93

KEY (CORRECT ANSWERS)

1. A		11. B	
2. B		12. C	
3. D		13. A	
4. C		14. D	
5. B		15. B	
6. A		16. D	
7. D		17. C	
8. D		18. B	
9. C		19. D	
10. A		20. A	

3 (#1)

SOLUTIONS TO PROBLEMS

1. ($40)(5/8) = $25

2. 27/64 = .421875 ≈ 42.188%

3. (36)(1 1/6) = 42

4. Let x = missing number. Then, 15 = .20x. Solving, x = 75

5. Let x = missing number. Then, x + 1/3 x = 96. Simplifying, 4/3 x = 96. Solving, x = 96 ÷ 4/3 = 72

6. .16 3/4 = 16 3/4% by simply moving the decimal point two places to the right.

7. (.55)(15) = 8.25

8. Let x = missing number. Then, x - 1/3 x = 96. Simplifying, 2/3 x = 96.
Solving, x = 96 ÷ 2/3 = 144

9. 15 3/4 ÷ 3 1/2 = 4.5 feet per footstool. The cost of one footstool is ($.245)(4.5) = $1.1025 ≈ $1.10

10. $907.99 ÷ 1231 = $.7376 per gallon. Since there are 16 half-pints in a gallon, the average cost per half-pint is $.7376 ÷ 16 ≈ $.046

11. (23)(9 3/4) = (23)(9.75) = 224.25 or 224 1/4

12. ($4.15)(3.45) = $14.3175 = $14.32

13. .0625 = 625/10,000 = 1/16

14. .03125 = 3125/100,000 = 1/32

15. 21.70 ÷ 1.75 = 12.4

16. The sum of these lunches is $1.354. Then, $1.354 ÷ 5 = $.2708 = $.271

17. $8.52 ÷ 12 = $.71 per dozen. Then, the cost of 5 dozen is ($.71)(5) = $3.55

18. 410.07 - 38.49 = 371.58

19. ($20.16)(7.75) = $156.24

20. 90.79 + 79.09 + 97.90 + 9.97 = 277.75

TEST 2

DIRECTIONS: Each question or incomplete statement is followed by several suggested answers or completions. Select the one that BEST answers the question or completes the statement. *PRINT THE LETTER OF THE CORRECT ANSWER IN THE SPACE AT THE RIGHT.*

1. 1600 is 40% of what number?
    A. 6400　　B. 3200　　C. 4000　　D. 5600

2. An executive's time card reads: Arrived 9:15 A.M., Left 2:05 P.M. How many hours was he in the office? _____ hours _____ minutes.
    A. 5; 10　　B. 4; 50　　C. 4; 10　　D. 5; 50

3. .4266 times .3333 will have the following number of decimals in the product:
    A. 8　　B. 4　　C. 1　　D. None of these

4. An office floor is 25 ft. wide by 36 ft. long. To cover this floor with carpet will require _____ square yards.
    A. 100　　B. 300　　C. 900　　D. 25

5. 1/8 of 1% expressed as a decimal is
    A. .125　　B. .0125　　C. 1.25　　D. .00125

6. $\dfrac{6 \div 4}{6 \times 4}$ equals 6x4
    A. 1/16　　B. 1　　C. 1/6　　D. 1/4

7. 1/25 of 230 equals
    A. 92.0　　B. 9.20　　C. .920　　D. 920

8. 4 times 3/8 equals
    A. 1 3/8　　B. 3/32　　C. 12.125　　D. 1.5

9. 3/4 divided by 4 equals
    A. 3　　B. 3/16　　C. 16/3　　D. 16

10. 6/7 divided by 2/7 equals
    A. 6　　B. 12/49　　C. 3　　D. 21

11. The interest on $240 for 90 days ' 6% is
    A. $4.80　　B. $3.40　　C. $4.20　　D. $3.60

12. 16 2/3% of 1728 is
    A. 91　　B. 288　　C. 282　　D. 280

13. 6 1/4% of 6400 is
   A. 2500 B. 410 C. 108 D. 400

14. 12 1/2% of 560 is
   A. 65 B. 40 C. 50 D. 70

15. 2 yards divided by 3 equals
   A. 2 feet B. 1/2 yard C. 3 yards D. 3 feet

16. A school has 540 pupils. 45% are boys. How many girls are there in this school?
   A. 243 B. 297 C. 493 D. 394

17. .1875 is equivalent to
   A. 18 3/4 B. 75/18 C. 18/75 D. 3/16

18. A kitchen cabinet listed at $42 is sold for $33.60. The discount allowed is
   A. 10% B. 15% C. 20% D. 30%

19. 3 6/8 divided by 8 1/4 equals
   A. 9 1/8 B. 12 C. 5/11 D. 243.16

20. An agent sold goods to the amount of $1480. His commission at 5 1/2% was
   A. $37.50 B. $81.40 C. 76.70 D. $81.10

KEY (CORRECT ANSWERS

1. C	11. D
2. B	12. B
3. A	13. D
4. A	14. D
5. D	15. A
6. A	16. B
7. B	17. D
8. D	18. C
9. B	19. C
10. C	20. B

3 (#2)

SOLUTIONS TO PROBLEMS

1. Let x = missing number. Then, 1600 = .40x. Solving, x = 4000

2. 2:05 PM - 9:15 AM = 4 hours 50 minutes

3. The product of two 4-decimal numbers is an 8-decimal number.

4. (25 ft)(36 ft) = 900 sq.ft. = 100 sq.yds.

5. (1/8)(1%) = (.125)(.01) = .00125

6. (6 ÷ 4) ÷ (6 x 4) = 3/2 ÷ 24 = (3/2)(1/24) = (1/16)

7. (1/25)(230) = 9.20

8. (4)(3/8) = 12/8 = 1.5

9. 3/4 ÷ 4 = (3/4)(1/4) = 3/16

10. 6/7 / 2/7 = (6/7)(7/2) = 3

11. ($240)(.06)(90/360) = $3.60

12. (16 2/3%)(1728) = (1/6)(1728) = 288

13. (6 1/4%)(6400) = (1/16)(6400) = 400

14. (12 1/2%)(560) = (1/8)(560) = 70

15. 2 yds ÷ 3 = 2/3 yds = (2/3)(3) = 2 ft.

16. If 45% are boys, then 55% are girls. Thus, (540)(.55) = 297

17. .1875 = 1875/10,000 = 3/16

18. $42 - $33.60 = $8.40.
    The discount is $8.40 ÷ $42 = .20 = 20%

19. 3 6/8 - 8 1/4 = (30/8)(4/33) = 5/11

20. ($1480)(.055) = $81.40

TEST 3

DIRECTIONS: Each question or incomplete statement is followed by several suggested answers or completions. Select the one that BEST answers the question or completes the statement. *PRINT THE LETTER OF THE CORRECT ANSWER IN THE SPACE AT THE RIGHT.*

1. 93.648 divided by 0.4 is

    A. 23.412   B. 234.12   C. 2.3412   D. 2341.2

    1._____

2. Add 4.3682, .0028, 34., 9.92, and from the sum subtract 1.992. The remainder is

    A. .46299   B. 4.6299   C. 462.99   D. 46.299

    2._____

3. At $2.88 per gross, three dozen will cost

    A. $8.64   B. $0.96   C. $0.72   D. $11.52

    3._____

4. 13 times 2.39 times 0.024 equals

    A. 745.68   B. 74.568   C. 7.4568   D. .74568

    4._____

5. A living room suite is marked $64 less 25 percent. A cash discount of 10 percent is allowed.
   The cash price is

    A. $53.20   B. $47.80   C. $36.00   D. $43.20

    5._____

6. 1/8 of 1 percent expressed as a decimal is

    A. .125   B. .0125   C. 1.25   D. .00125

    6._____

7. 16 percent of 482.11 equals

    A. 77.1376   B. 771.4240   C. 7714.2400   D. 7.71424

    7._____

8. A merchant sold a chair for $60. This was at a profit of 25 percent of what it cost him. The chair cost him

    A. $48   B. $45   C. $15   D. $75

    8._____

9. Add 5 hours 13 minutes, 3 hours 49 minutes, and 14 minutes. The sum is _____ hours _____ minutes.

    A. 9; 16   B. 9;76   C. 8;16   D. 8;6

    9._____

10. 89 percent of $482 is

    A. $428.98   B. $472.36   C. $42.90   D. $47.24

    10._____

11. 200 percent of 800 is

    A. 16   B. 1600   C. 2500   D. 4

    11._____

12. Add 2 feet 3 inches, 4 feet 11 inches, 8 inches, 6 feet 6 inches. The sum is _____ feet _____ inches.

    A. 12; 4   B. 12; 14   C. 14; 4   D. 14; 28

    12._____

13. A merchant bought dresses at $15 each and sold them at $20 each. His overhead expenses are 20 percent of cost. His net profit on each dress is

    A. $1
    B. $2
    C. $3
    D. $4

14. 0.0325 expressed as a percent is

    A. 325%
    B. 3 1/4%
    C. 32 1/2%
    D. 32.5%

15. Add 3/4, 1/8, 1/32, 1/2; and from the sum subtract 4/8. The remainder is

    A. 2/32
    B. 7/8
    C. 29/32
    D. 3/4

16. A salesman gets a commission of 4 percent on his sales. If he wants his commission to amount to $40, he will have to sell merchandise totaling

    A. $160
    B. $10
    C. $1,000
    D. $100

17. Jones borrowed $225,000 for five years at 3 1/2 percent. The annual interest charge was

    A. $1,575
    B. $1,555
    C. $7,875
    D. $39,375

18. A kitchen cabinet listed at $42 is sold for $33.60. The discount allowed is _____ percent.

    A. 10
    B. 15
    C. 20
    D. 30

19. The exact number of days from May 5, 2007 to July 1, 2007 is _____ days.

    A. 59
    B. 58
    C. 56
    D. 57

20. A dealer sells an article at a loss of 50% of the cost. Based on the selling price, the loss is

    A. 25%
    B. 50%
    C. 100%
    D. none of these

KEY (CORRECT ANSWERS)

1. B
2. D
3. C
4. D
5. D
6. D
7. A
8. A
9. A
10. A
11. B
12. C
13. B
14. B
15. C
16. C
17. C
18. C
19. D
20. C

SOLUTIONS TO PROBLEMS

1. 93.648 ÷ .4 = 234.12

2. 4.368 + .0028 + 34 + 9.92 - 1.992 = 48.291 - 1.992 = 46.299

3. $2.88 for 12 dozen means $.24 per dozen. Three dozen will cost (3)($.24) = $.72

4. (13)(2.39)(.024) = .74568

5. ($64)(.75)(.90) = $43.20

6. (1/8)(1%) = (.125)(.01) = .00125

7. (.16)(482.11) = 77.1376

8. Let x = cost. Then, 1.25x = $60. Solving, x = $48

9. 5 hrs. 13 min. + 3 hrs. 49 min. + 14 min = 8 hrs. 76 min.

10. (.89)($482) = $428.98

11. 200% = 2. So, (200%)(800) = (2)(800) = 1600

12. 2 ft. 3 in. + 4 ft. 11 in. + 8 in. + 6 ft. 6 in. + 12 ft. 28 in. = 14 ft. 4 in.

13. Overhead is (.20)($15) = $3. The net profit is $20 - $15 - $3 = $2

14. .0325 = 3.25% = 3 1/4%

15. 3/4 + 1/8 + 1/32 + 1/2 - 4/8 = 45/32 - 4/8 = 29/32

16. Let x = sales. Then, $40 = .04$x$. Solving, x = $1000

17. Annual interest is ($225,000)(.035) x 1 = 7875

18. $42 - $33.60 = $8.40. Then, $8.40 ÷ $42 = .20 = 20%

19. The number of days left for May, June, July is 26, 30, and 1. Thus, 26 + 30 + 1 = 57

20. Let x = cost, so that .50x = selling price. The loss is represented by .50x ÷ .50x = 1 = 100% on the selling price. (Note: The loss in dollars is x - .50x = .50x)

MEASUREMENT RELATIONSHIPS AND PRINCIPLES

1. ENGLISH MEASUREMENT

    <u>Common English Measures</u>

    Length
    1 foot (ft) = 12 inches (in)
    1 yard (yd) = 3 feet (ft)
    1 mile (mi) = 5,280 feet (ft)

    Volume
    1 quart (qt) = 2 pints (pt)
    1 gallon (gal) = 4 quarts (qts)

    Weight
    1 pound (lb) = 16 ounces (oz)
    1 ton = 2,000 pounds (lb)

    Time
    1 minute (min) = 60 seconds (sec)
    1 hour (hr) = 60 minutes (min)
    1 day (da) = 24 hours (hr)
    1 week (wk) = 7 days (da)
    1 year (yr) = 52 weeks (wk) = 365 days (da)

The equivalent measures in the table above should be memorized. Once committed to memory, only an additional knowledge of basic arithmetic is necessary for solving most commonly encountered test problems.

<u>Problem:</u>   Change 38 yards to feet

<u>Solution:</u>   1 yard = 3 feet
38 · 1 yard = 38·3 feet
38 yards = 114 feet

<u>Problem:</u>   How many pints are in 8 1/2 gallons:

<u>Solution:</u>   1 gallon = 4 quarts
8 1/2 x 1 gallon = 8 1/2 x 4 quarts
8 1/2 gallons = 34 quarts
1 quart = 2 pints
34 x 1 quart = 34 x 2 pints
34 quarts = 68 pints
Thus, 8 1/2 gallons = 34 quarts = 68 pints,
so 8 1/2 gallons = 68 pints.

<u>Problem:</u>   A man drives 10 miles in 20 minutes. What was his speed in miles per hour?

<u>Solution:</u> $\dfrac{10 \text{ miles}}{20 \text{ minutes}} \times \dfrac{\overset{3}{60} \text{ minutes}}{1 \text{ hour}}$

$= \dfrac{30 \text{ miles}}{1 \text{ hour}} = 30 \text{ miles per hour}$

Notice how *miles per minute* was converted to *miles per hour*. We multiplied by the unit ratio *60 min/1 hr* (which is like multiplying by an equivalent of $^V(I)$ to cancel the minutes and replace them with *hour*. This is a common technique when miles per hour, cost per pound, and similar ratios are involved.

Problem: The speed of sound is approximately 1,100 feet per second. How many miles per hour is this?

Solution:
$$\frac{1100 \text{ feet}}{1 \text{ second}} \times \frac{3600 \text{ second}}{1 \text{ hour}} \times \frac{1 \text{ mile}}{5280 \text{ feet}}$$

$$= \frac{1100 \times 3600}{5280} \frac{\text{mile}}{\text{hour}}$$

750 miles per hour

Here we multiplied by two unit ratios, $\frac{3600 \text{ seconds}}{1 \text{ hour}}$ and $\frac{1 \text{ mile}}{5280 \text{ feet}}$ expressly designed to replace *seconds* by *hours* and *feet* by *miles*. Notice that each of these ratios alone is the equivalent of 1.

Problem: Ten feet of pipe sell for $13.77. At this rate, how much would ten yards cost?

Solution: Since 1 yard = 3 feet, 10 yards = 30 feet. A 10-foot unit sells for $13.77. For 30 feet we need 3 10-foot units: 3 x 13.77 = $41.41

Problem: Assume coffee costs about $4 per pound. Is this more or less than the cost per pound of a new car which sells for $10,000 and weighs 2.3 tons?

Solution:
$$\frac{\overset{5}{10{,}000} \text{ dollars}}{2.3 \text{ tons}} \times \frac{1 \text{ ton}}{2000 \text{ lbs}}$$

$$= \frac{5 \text{ dollars}}{2.3 \text{ lbs}}$$

= $2.18/pound

Here again, in order to solve the problem we multiplied by the equivalent of 1.

The new car costs less per pound than the coffee.

Problem: A recycling center pays 12¢ for every 50 pounds of old newspapers. How much do they pay per ton? 40

Solution: $$\frac{12¢}{50 \text{ lbs}} \times \frac{2000 \text{ lbs}}{1 \text{ ton}}$$

$$= \frac{480¢}{\text{ton}} = \$4.80 \text{ per ton}$$

EXERCISES

1. A glacier moves at a rate of 18 inches per year. How many feet will it move in 25 years?

2. Assume that a gallon of water weighs 8 pounds. What is the weight in tons of the water in a swimming pool that holds 60,000 gallons?

3. Kathy drives 8 miles in 12 minutes. What is her speed in miles per hour?

4. Julio needs 56 yards of white pine boards. These boards sell for 40c per foot. How much will 56 yards cost?

5. A can of cat food holds 6 ounces. How many cans would you need to buy in order to purchase 10 pounds of cat food?

6. A person is 81 inches tall. How many feet tall is this?

7. Four feet of fabric cost $15. At the same rate, how much would you pay for 13 yards of the fabric?

8. You have 10 ropes, each 10 feet in length. How many 9-inch lengths can you get from these 10 ropes?

9. An experiment requires 1/2 pint per student of a certain chemical during a chemistry laboratory. The chemical is sold by the gallon only. How many gallons should be on hand for a class of 43 students?

2. METRIC MEASUREMENT

Common Metric Measures

Length
1 meter (m) = 1000 millimeters (mm)
1 meter (m) = 100 centimeters (cm)
1 kilometer (km) = 1000 meters (m)

Volume
1 liter (l) = 1000 milliliters (ml)

Weight
1 gram (g) = 1000 milligrams (mg)
1 kilogram (kg) = 1000 grams (g)

The information in this table should be memorized. It is helpful to know that the metric system has a well-designed system of prefixes:

kilo means 1000
centi means 1/100
milli means 1/1000

Thus, *kilometer* means *1000 meters*. *Centimeter* means *1/100 of a meter*, so it follows that 100 centimeters make up 1 meter. *Milli* means 1/1000. Thus, a millimeter is 1/1000 of a meter; a milliliter is 1/1000 of a liter; a millogram is 1/1000 of a gram. This is the same as saying that 1000 millimeters equal
1 meter; 1000 milliliters equal 1 liter; 1000 milligrams equal 1 gram.

If there were a metric unit called a *boron,* then a kiloboron would equal 1000 borons, a centiboron would be 1/100 of a boron, and a milliboron would be 1/1000 of a boron. How many milli-borons would it take to make one boron?
The rest of this section is devoted to conversions and problem solving within the metric system.

Problem: Change 250 centimeters to meters.

Solution: 1 centimeter = 1/100 meter = .01 meter
                So, 250 cm = 250 .01 m
                250 cm = 2.50 m

The preceding example illustrates an important point: Nearly all metric conversions can be accomplished by moving a decimal point. Since centimeters and meters are related by 1/100 or 100, the decimal point moves two places - to the left for centimeters to meters (moving from a smaller unit to a larger one) and to the right for meters to centimeters (moving from a larger unit to a smaller unit).

    centimeters - → meters: 476 cm = 4.75 m
    meters - → centimeters: 3.6 m = 360 cm

Note that the decimal point moves to the left when converting from smaller to larger units. It moves right when converting from larger to smaller units.
How many places would you move the decimal point for meter/ millimeter conversions? Since 1 meter = 1000 millimeters (or 1 millimeter = 1/1000 meter), the decimal point moves 3 places.

    millimeters - → meters: 3700 mm = 3.7 m
    meters - → milliliters: .5 m = 500 mm

Likewise,

    milliliters - → liters: 260 ml = .26 l
    liters - → milliliters: 3.71 l = 3710 ml
    milligrams - → grams: 34.6 mg = .0346 g
    grams - → milligrams: 34 g = 34000 mg

How about meter/kilometer conversions or gram/kilogram conversions? Since a kilometer equals 1000 meters and a kilogram equals 1000 grams, the conversions also involve multiplying or dividing by 1000, that is, by moving the decimal point 3 places.

    meter - → kilometer: 3500 m = 3.500 km
    kilometer - → meter: .25 km = 250 m
    gram - → kilogram: 200 g = .2 kg

5

        kilogram → gram: 1.5 kg = 1500 g

Problem: Change 2.6 centimeters to millimeters.
Solution: According to the metric table,
                100 cm = 1 m = 1000 mm
                Thus, 1 cm = 10 mm
                But if 1 cm = 10 mm,
                then, 2.6 cm = 26 mm.

(Notice, again, that you only need to move the decimal point. You move it one place this time since centimeters and millimeters are related by a factor of 10 or by a factor of 1/10, depending on the direction of the change.)

EXERCISES

10. A bottle holds 0.3 liters. How many milliliters is this?

11. A can of pineapples weighs 400 grams. How many kilograms is this? How many milligrams?

12. Paul is 1.7 m tall. What is his height in cm?

13. A glacier moves at the rate of 31 cm per year. How many meters will it move in a century?

14. At a cost of 32¢ for 5 grams, how much would you pay for half a kilogram?

15. How many 15 cm lengths can be cut from a strand of material 3 m long?

16. How many 750 ml wine bottles will it take to exceed the contents of 7 bottles each holding 1 liter?

17. When nerves are severed and then reattached on the operating table, they regenerate themselves at the rate of 1 mm/day. Dan cut his forearm at a point 21.5 cm from his fingertips. How many days after surgery will it be before sensation returns to his fingertips?

18. At a rate of $42/m, what would be the total cost of paving a stretch of road which is 3.6 km long?

19. Paul is charged $3.20 for 250 ml of a particular medicine. If he takes two ml doses per day, what
    a. is his approximate cost per day?
    b. is the cost of 4 liters of this medicine?

3. ENGLISH AND METRIC MEASUREMENTS

Most people are familiar with the relative sizes and uses of the common English measures discussed in Section 1 above. This section includes some exercises involving English measures but the discussion that follows will focus on the less familiar metric units.

A <u>meter</u> is slightly longer than a yard. A person who is two meters tall is looked up to by most people. A <u>centimeter</u> is 1/100 of a meter and forms the major subdivisions on a meter-stick. The width of the fingernail on your little finger is probably about 1 cm. A pencil is slightly less than 1 cm in diameter. A <u>millimeter</u> is 1/10 the size of a centimeter and is roughly equal to the thickness of a dime. A <u>kilometer</u> (1000 meters) is slightly more than 1/2 mile (1 km roughly equals 5/8 miles).

A <u>liter</u> is roughly the same as a quart. A <u>milliliter,</u> is one thousand times smaller. Wine is often sold in 750 ml bottles (which are the same as 0.75 1 bottles). A teaspoon holds about 5 ml.

The basic metric unit of weight, 1 gram, is roughly the weight of a paperclip. As a rule, only light objects have their weights expressed in grams. A candy bar might weigh 30 grams. Far more common are <u>kilogram</u> weights. A kilogram is more than 2 pounds. A 220-pound football player weighs 100 kilograms. However, human weights of 50, 60, 70, and 80 kg are more common. Conversely, <u>milligram</u> weights are very small; they are most often encountered in scientific fields.

The metric unit of temperature is the <u>degree Celsius.</u> Water freezes at $^\circ$ C and boils at 100° C. A comfortable outdoor temperature is somewhere in the upper 20° C. Normal body temperature is about 37° C.

<u>EXERCISES</u>

20. For each of the following items, identify the approximate measurement from the choices given.

    a. Family car (feet): 3, 7, 14, 28
    b. Arm length (feet): 1, 3, 6, 12
    c. Big toe width (inches): 1/2, 1, 1 1/2, 2
    d. Record album width (inches): 2, 4, 12, 24
    e. Pitcher of beer (quarts): 1, 2, 4, 8
    f. Table height (inches): 10, 30, 50, 70
    g. Gallon of milk (pounds): 1, 2, 8, 16
    h. New York to Chicago (miles): 100, 400, 800, 1,600
    i. Can of soda (ounces): 4, 8, 12, 18

21. Which metric unit is most likely to be used in measuring the following?

    a. Width of a front door
    b. Volume of a large jug of wine
    c. Weight of a hamburger or hotdog
    d. Distance from a suburban house to the edge of the property line
    e. Distance from Hartford, Connecticut, to New Haven, Connecticut
    f. Weight of a bowling ball
    g. Height of a basketball player
    h. Your weight
    i. Diameter of a dime
    j. Length of the Mississippi River
    k. Weight of a dime

l. Width of camera film
m. Weight of ten grains of sand
n. Weight of a can of peach slices
o. Volume of a soda can

22. For each of the following items, identify the most likely approximate measurement from the choices given.

   a. Pencil length (cm): 0.5, 2, 20, 35, 70
   b. Volume of coffee cup (ml): 250, 500, 750, 1000, 1500
   c. Newborn baby's weight (kg): 1, 3.5, 8, 12, 20
   d. Automobile gasoline purchase (1): 1, 4, 20, 40, 120
   e. Volume of soda can (ml): 10, 35, 350, 700, 1500
   f. Length of a football field (m): 10, 50, 90, 130, 170
   g. Tablespoon of medicine (ml): 1, 5, 50, 500, 5000
   h. Temperature on a hot summer day (°C): 38°, 48°, 58°, 68°, 78°
   i. Temperature cool enough for a sweater (°C): 6°, 16°, 26°, 36°, 46°
   j. Outdoor iceskating temperature (°C): -8°, 8°, 18°, 28°, 38°

4. CALIBRATED SCALES

Every readable scale has markings on it. Some of the markings will be labeled and, very likely, some won't. To read the scale, you must understand what the markings represent. With this information, you can determine the reading on the gauge.

Problem: What is the reading on this gauge?

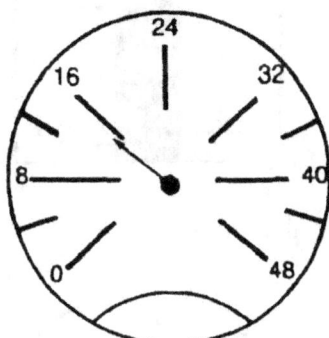

Solution: The longer scale markings represent multiples of 8, as labeled. The shorter markings are half-way between the longer ones. Thus, for example, the marking halfway between 8 and 16 represents 8 + 4 or 12. The pointer on the gauge lies between 12 and 16, but appears to be closer to 16 than to 12. The reading is approximately 15.

Problem: What reading is the arrow pointing to on this gauge?

8

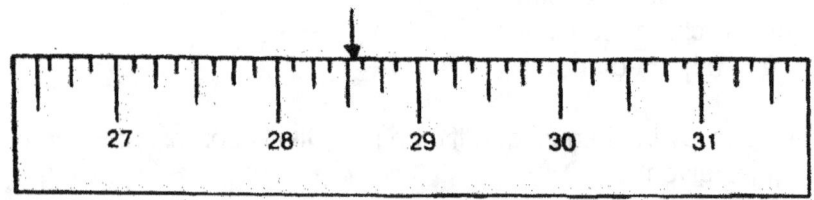

Solution: Here the long markings are marked off in increasing units of 1. Therefore, the next longest markings represent 1/2 units and the next longest 1/4 units; the shortest markings are half-way between 1/4 units and must represent 1/8 units. The arrow lies between 28 1/2 and 28 5/8. Since 1/2 = 4/8, the arrow lies half-way between the 1/8 unit markings. Half of 1/8 is 1/16. Thus, the reading is 28 1/2 + 1/16 = 28 8/16 + 1/16 = 28 9/16.

When reading gauges, be sure to figure out what the markings represent before you try to decipher the reading. Be careful, too. On some gauges the readings decrease as you move from left to right or from bottom to top.

EXERCISES

23. What is the approximate reading on this gauge?

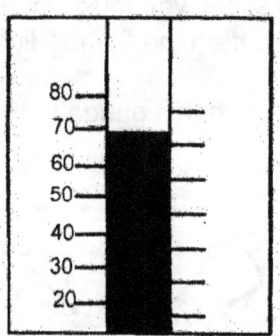

24. Estimate the reading on this gauge.

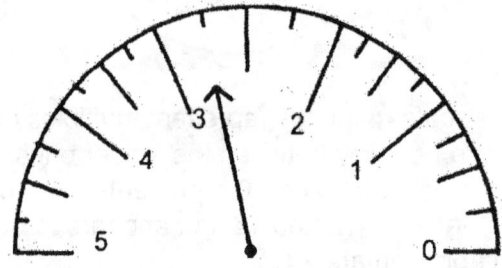

25. What is the reading on this gauge?

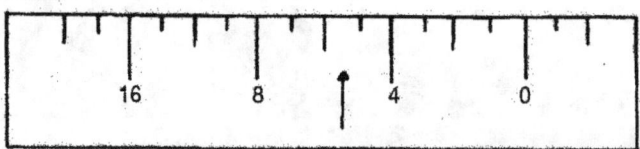

26. Read this scale.

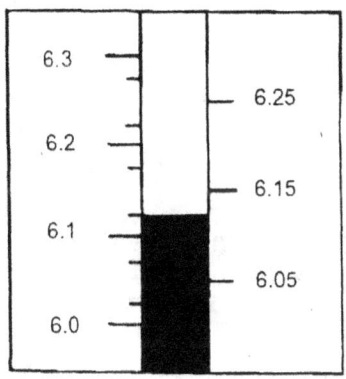

27. What measures are arrows a, b, c pointing to on this ruler?

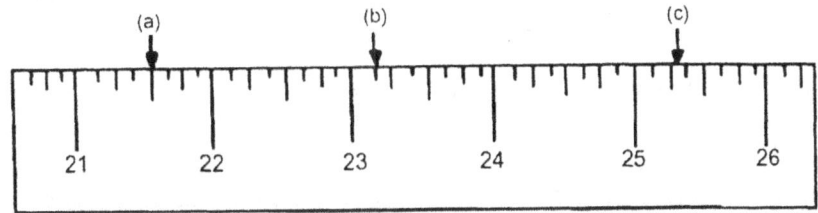

28. The pointer on this dial reads approximately

A. 28 B. 0.23 C. 0.27 D. 0.31

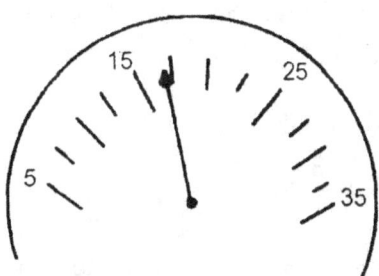

KEY (CORRECT ANSWERS)

1. 18 inches per year = 1 1/2 feet per year.

   1 1/2 x 25 = 25 + 12 1/2 = 37 1/2 feet in 25 years

2. 60,000 gal x 8 lbs/gal = 480,000 pounds of water
   480,000 lbs ÷ 2000 lbs/ton = 240 tons of water

3. $\dfrac{8 \text{ miles}}{12 \text{ minutes}} \times \dfrac{\overset{5}{60} \text{ minutes}}{1 \text{ hour}} = \dfrac{40 \text{ miles}}{1 \text{ hour}}$ = 40 miles per hour

   Alternatively: 12 minutes = 1/5 hour so she drove 8 miles in 1/5 hour. So, in one hour she would drive 40 miles or 40 miles per hour.

4. 56 yards = 168 feet. 168 feet x 40¢/foot = 6720¢
   56 yards cost $67.20

5. 10 lbs x 16 oz/lb = 160 oz   160 ÷ 6 = 25 2/3. You would need to buy 27 cans of cat food.

6. 81 ÷ 12 = 6 9/12 = 6 3/4 feet

7. One foot cost $15/4 = $3.75. Thus, 13 yards = 39 feet and cost $3.75 x 39 or $146.25.

8. The answer is 130. Each rope is 120 inches long. Since 120 ÷ 9 = 13 1/3, we can get 13 9-inch lengths from each rope. The extra 1/3 inch is unusable. We have 10 ropes so we can get 130 9-inch lengths altogether.

9. We need 43 half pints or 43/2 pints.

   $\dfrac{43}{2} \text{ pints} \cdot \dfrac{1 \text{ quart}}{2 \text{ pints}} \cdot \dfrac{1 \text{ gal}}{4 \text{ quarts}} = \dfrac{43}{16} \text{ gal}$

   = 2 11/16 gal. Since only whole gallons are available, we need 3 gallons.

10. 300 ml

11. 0.4 kg

12. 170 cm

13. 3100 cm per century. 31 m per century.

14. 1/2 kg = 500 grams. There are 100 5-gram units in 500 grams.
    Thus, you would pay .32 . 100 = $32.

15. 3m = 300 cm   300 ÷ 15 = 20 15-cm lengths

16. 7 bottles @ 1 liter each = 7 liters = 7000 ml
    7000 ÷ 750 = 9.3
    So, 10 bottles would be needed to exceed 7000 ml

17. 21.5 cm = 215 mm. Thus, the predicted recovery time is 215 days.

18. $\frac{\$42}{m} \cdot \frac{1000 m}{1 km}$ = $42000 per km. Thus, for 3.6 km, the cost is $42,000 x 3.6 = $151,200

19. (a) 250/4 = 125/2 = 62 1/2 doses per bottle.
    $3.20 v 125/2 = $3.20 x 2/125 = $6.40/125 or approximately
    $.05. Thus, each 4-ml dose costs about 5c. Since Paul takes 2 per day, his daily
    cost is about 10¢.

    (b) 4 l = 4000 ml. 4000 * 250 = 16 so there are 16 250-ml amounts in 4 l. Since each
    250-ml amount cost $3.20, 4 l would cost $3.20 x 16 = $51.20

20. a. 14   d. 12   g. 8
    b. 3   e. 2   h. 800
    c. 1   f. 30   i. 12

21. a. m   f. kg   k. gm
    b. l   g. m   l. mm (e.g., 35 mm film)
    c. gm   h. kg   m. mg
    d. m   i. mm or cm   n. g
    e. km   j. km   o. ml

22. a. 20   e. 350   h. 38°
    b. 250   f. 90   i. 16°
    c. 3.5   g. 5   j. -8°
    d. 40

23. 68

24. 17

25. 5.5

26. 6.125

27. a. 21 1/2   b. 23 1/8   c. 25 5/16

28. c

Food Preparation-Handling and Storage

1. FOOD PREPARATION

    Begin with clean, fresh food. Handle food only when necessary.

    Don't dip fingers into food or use a stirring spoon to taste.

    Use oysters, clams and other frozen foods, fluid milk products and frozen milk desserts from approved sources.

    Never lean or sit on work surfaces.

    Foods should never be prepared in yards, alleys, stairs or hallways.

    Keep food that is on display covered so it can't be touched or coughed on by customers or contaminated by flies and other bugs.

    Always follow the recipe. Cook custards and cream sauces well. Chill them at once.

    Wash thoroughly with brush and clean water all vegetables and fruits which are to be served raw.

    As a food safeguard, boil leftover vegetables, gravies, soups, and other liquid foods before serving.

    Make sure that all mixing, grinding and chopping machines are thoroughly cleaned after each use. In order to properly clean one of these machines, one should know how to take it apart and assemble it.

    Work only in a well-lighted area that is well-ventilated.

2. FOOD STORAGE AND HANDLING

    Food should be stored well off the floor, away from walls or dripping pipes.

    Keep all food, bulk or otherwise, covered and safe from contamination.

    Check food daily and throw away any spoiled or dirty food.

    Store cleaning, disinfection, insect and rodent-killing powders and liquids away from foods, PLAINLY MARKED.

    Keep foods in refrigerator at temperature of 45° F or below.

    Check the temperature regularly with a good thermometer.

    Keep all cooling compartments closed except when you're using them.

    Store food in a refrigerator in such a way that inside air can circulate freely.

    Always refrigerate meats, creamed foods and custard desserts.

    Keep all refrigerated foods covered, and use up stored leftovers quickly.

    When dishes and utensils are sparkling clean, keep them that way by proper storage. Keep all cups and glasses inverted.

    Cakes, doughnuts and fruit pies may be kept inside a covered display area.

    The only goods that should be left on the counter uncovered are those which are wrapped and do not contain anything which could spoil at room temperature.

    Don't set dirty dishes, pots, cartons or boxes on food tables.

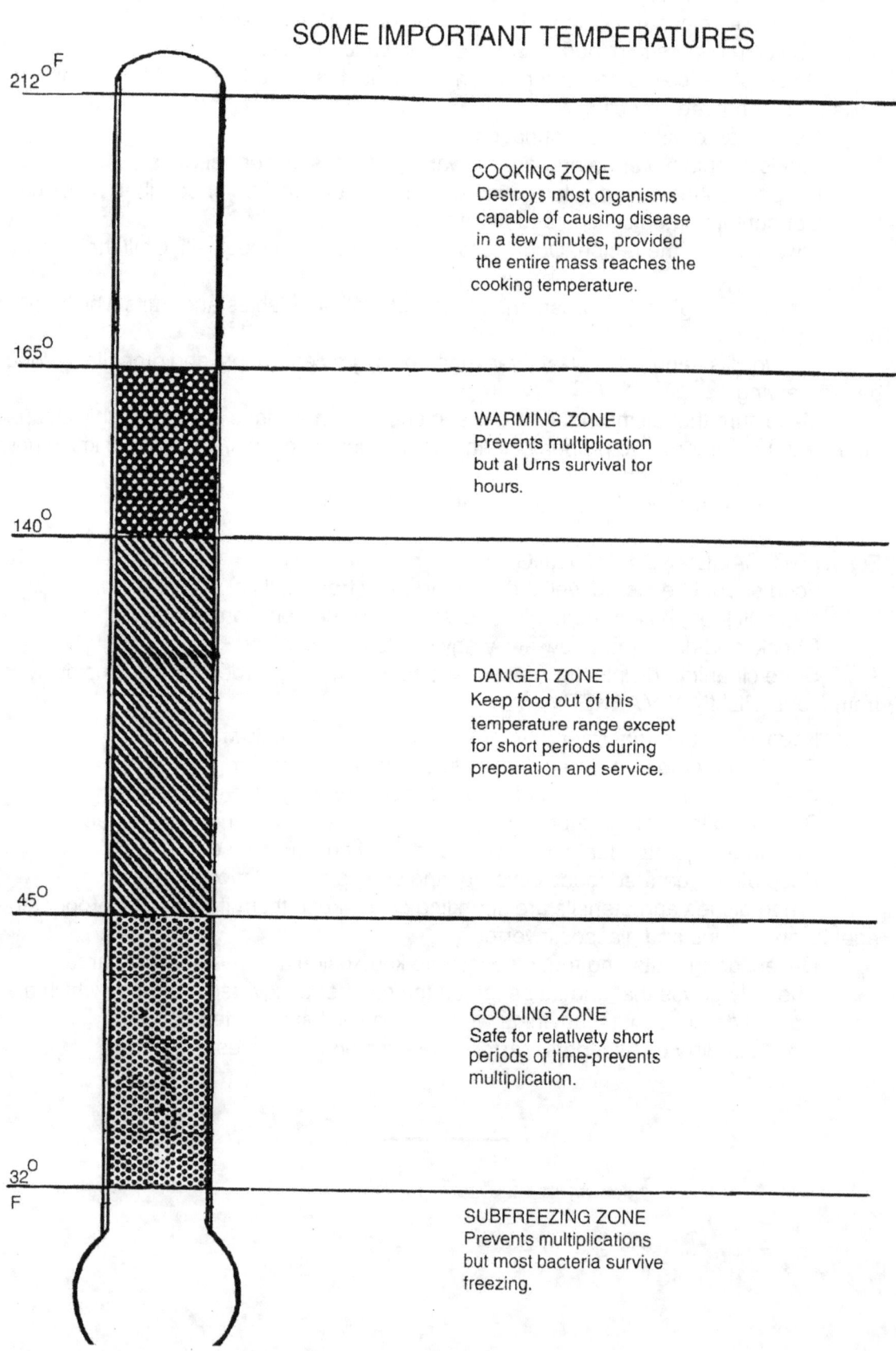

TEMPERATURE RANGE FOR SAFE STORAGE OF FOODS

Zone I   Sub-freezing temperatures $0°$ F to $-15°$ F ($-18°$ to $-9.4°$ C)

  A. Frozen meat, fish, and vegetables
  B. Frozen fruits
  C. Ice Cream
  D. Homemade frozen deserts

Zone II   High Humidity (85%) and Moderate Air Circulation $34°$ to $37°$ F ($1.1°$ to $2.7°$ C)

  A. Fresh meat, chicken, and fish
  B. Sliced smoked ham and bacon
  C. Sliced cold cuts of meat
  D. Leftover canned and cooked meat

Zone III $38°$ to $40°$ F ($3.3°$ to $4.4°$ C)

  A. Fresh milk, cream, and buttermilk
  B. Cottage cheese and butter (both covered)
  C. Fresh orange and tomato juice (covered)
  D. Bottled beverage (for chilling)

Zone IV $40°$ to $43°$ F ($4.4°$ to $6.1°$ C) Moderate Humidity

  A. Berries, pears, and peaches
  B. Ripe grapefruit and oranges
  C. Ripe tomatoes (short time only)
  D. Fresh eggs
  E. Margarine
  F. Custards and puddings (day or two only)
  G. Prepared salads (for chilling)

Zone V $40°$ to $45°$ F ($4.4°$ to $7.2°$ C) High Humidity

  A. Cherries and cranberries
  B. Lettuce and celery
  C. Spinach, kale, and other greens
  D. Beets, carrots, parsnips, and turnips
  E. Peas and lima beans
  F. Cucumbers and eggplant (short time only)

Zone VI $55°$ to $60°$ F ($12.7°$ to $15.1°$ C) Fairly High Humidity and Moderate Circulation. (Good Fruit Cellar or Storage Cellar Well Ventilated).

  A. Apples, cabbage, potatoes, pumpkin, squash, unripened tomatoes, and maple syrup (in tight container)

Zone VII   Normal Room Temperature. Dry Storage
   A.   Ready prepared cereals
   B.   Crackers
   C.   Bottled beverages

Zone VIII   Normal Room Temperature Storage

   A.   Peanut Butter and honey
   B.   Salad oils and vegetable shortenings
   C.   Catsup and pickles
   D.   Jelly and preserves
   E.   Dried fruits and bananas (short time)
   F.   Flour
   G.   Dried peas and beans
   H.   Sugar and salt

MICROBIOLOGY OF FOODS: BACTERIA

In order to understand the reasons behind food sanitation practices, it is necessary to know a few facts about the microorganisms which cause food spoilage and foodborne disease.

Bacteria, commonly called germs, are extremely small, plant-like organisms which must be viewed through a microscope in order to be seen. If 25,000,000 bacteria were placed in a line, that line would be only one inch long; one million could fit on the head of a pin. Like any living thing, bacteria require food, moisture, and the proper temperature for growth. Most of them need air, but some can thrive only in the absence of air (these are called anaerobic) and some can grow with or without air (facultative). Bacteria are found everywhere on the earth, in the air, and in the water. Soil abounds with bacteria which grow on dead organic matter.

SHAPES OF BACTERIA

One method of classifying bacteria is by their shape. All bacteria can be assigned to one of the following categories.

A. Cocci (plural of coccus) are round or spherical in shape. While they are able to live alone, they often exist in groups. Single chains are called streptococci. Those which form a grape-like cluster are called staphylococci, while those that form pairs are called diplococci. Some bacteria are named after the portion of the human anatomy they infect; for example, pneumococci infect the lungs, enterococci infect the intestines, and meningococci infect the meninges (protective sheath around the brain). Some of the common diseases caused by the cocci group are pneumonia, septic sore throat, scarlet fever, and meningitis.

B. Bacilli (plural of bacillus) are rod-shaped. Some of these also congregate in the single chain form, and are called streptobacilli. Some common diseases caused by bacilli are typhoid fever, tuberculosis, and anthrax.

C. Spirilla (plural of spirillum) are spiral or comma-shaped. Diseases caused by spirilla include cholera and syphilis.

SPORES

Some bacilli are able to protect themselves under adverse conditions by forming a protective shell or wall around themselves; in this form they are in the non-vegetative stage and are called spores. These bacterial spores can be likened to the seeds of a plant which are also resistant to adverse conditions. During the spore stage, bacteria do not reproduce or multiply. As soon as these spores find themselves under proper conditions of warmth, moisture, food and possibly air requirements. they resume their normal (vegetative) stage, and resume their growth. Since spores are designed to withstand rigorous conditions, they are difficult to destroy by the normal methods. Much higher killing temperatures and longer time periods are required. Fortunately, there are only a relatively few pathogenic or disease-causing bacilli which are spore formers. Tetanus, anthrax, and botulism are diseases caused by spore formers.

BACTERIAL REPRODUCTION

Bacteria reproduce by splitting in two, this is called binary fission. For this reason, their numbers are always doubling: one bacterium generates two; each of these generates two, resulting in a new total of four: etc. The time it takes for bacteria to double (generation time) is roughly fifteen to thirty minutes under good conditions.

TYPES OF BACTERIA ACCORDING TO THEIR EFFECT ON MAN

Types of bacteria, classified according to their effect on us, are:

    A. Harmful or disease-producing
    B. Undesirable
    C. Beneficial
    D. Benign

    A. Harmful or disease-producing bacteria are known as pathogenic bacteria or pathogens. They cause various diseases of man, animals, and plants.

    B. Undesirable bacteria, which cause decomposition of foods, are often referred to as putrefying bacteria. Bacteria that act on sugars in food, resulting in souring, are called saccharolytic bacteria.

    C. Beneficial bacteria are used in the production of various foods, including cultured milk, yogurt, cheese, and sauerkraut.

The large intestine, or colon, contains millions of bacteria which are normal inhabitants of the intestinal tract, and we call this type *"coliform"* bacteria. It can be seen, therefore, that where coliform bacteria are found in food or water, they are an indication of fecal contamination. The coliforms themselves are not pathogenic, but where fecal contamination occurs, it is probable that other pathogenic organisms from the intestine may be present. The presence of coliform bacteria is often used as an index of good or bad sanitary practices.

Bacteria are essential in the operation of certain sewage disposal plants, known as *"activated sludge plants"*. In these plants the bacteria digest the organic sewage and either liquefy the solid matter which is in colloid form, or change it so that it settles out.

The greatest number of bacteria are found in the soil where they thrive on dead organic matter. They are constantly decomposing it, so that eventually it is changed into an inorganic form. This essential process of nature makes it possible for plants to absorb inorganic nutriment. Other types of bacteria *"fix"* nitrogen from the air, forming nitrates in the soil, generally on the roots of legumes.

    D. Benign bacteria, as far as we know at the present time, are neither helpful nor harmful to man. Of the hundreds of thousands of strains of bacteria, most fall into this category.

It must be realized that may bacteria are essential in the balance of nature, and the destruction of all bacteria in the world would be catastrophic. Our main objective in public health protection, in which food handling plays a vital role, is the control and destruction of the pathogenic bacteria and those that cause food spoilage.

CONDITIONS FOR GROWTH

    A. Food - Bacterial require food for growth. Food must be absorbed in liquid form through the cell wall of the organism. Generally bacteria prefer neutral foods (ph 6-8) but some can thrive on highly acid or alkaline media.

    B. Moisture - Moisture (water) is an essential requirement. If moisture is not present, bacteria will not multiply and eventually may die. Processes which depend on removing available water, i.e., water in liquid form, from bacteria are used to preserve foods. Such methods include dehydration, freezing, and preserving in salt or sugar.

    C. Temperature - In general, bacteria prefer a warm temperature and grow best between 90-100° F. (Optimum temperature) The temperature of the body, 98.6° F, is excellent for bacterial growth; when bacteria are cultured in the laboratory, they are kept at this temperature. However, different types of bacteria prefer different temperatures, and are as follows:

<u>Mesophilic</u>: Grow best at temperatures between 50-110° F. Most bacteria are in this group.

Thermophilic: Love heat. These grow best at temperatures between 110-150° F. or more

Psychrophilic: Love cold. These grow best at temperatures below 50° F.

Where heat is employed to destroy pathogenic bacteria, the food processor often must contend with thermophilic or thermoduric bacteria, which may withstand the pasteurizing or sterilizing processes. These bacteria are not pathogenic, but may be putrefactive.

D. Air - With respect to air atmospheric oxygen, we find that some bacteria can grow only where air is present; these are called aerobes. Some bacteria can grow only in a medium where air is absent, and these are called anaerobes. They can thrive in a sealed can, jar, or bottle of food. Those bacteria which prefer to live where air is present but may grow without air are termed facultative aerobes, and those which prefer to grow in the absence of air but may grow where air is present are called facultative anaerobes.

LOCOMOTION

Bacteria cannot crawl, fly, or move about. A few types do have thread-like appendages called flagella, with which they can propel themselves to a very limited extent. Therefore, they must be carried from place to place by some vehicle or through some channel. The channels of transmission include: air, water, food, hands, coughing, sneezing, insects, rodents, dirty equipment, unsafe plumbing connections, and unclean utensils. Hands are one of the most dangerous vehicles. There is no doubt that better care of food handlers' hands would aid greatly in cutting down the transmission of disease.

DESTRUCTION BY HEAT

The most reliable and time-tested method of destroying bacteria is heat. This method is effective only when both time and temperature factors are applied. In other words, not only do we have to reach the desired temperature to kill bacteria, but we must allow sufficient time to permit the heat to kill the more sturdy members. The lower the temperature (to certain limits, of course) the longer the time required to kill bacteria. Conversely, the higher the temperature, the less time is necessary. An example of this principle involves the two accepted methods for pasteurizing milk. In the *"holding"* method, milk is held at a temperature of 145° F for thirty minutes. In the more recently developed *"flash"* or *"high temperature-short time"* method, milk is held at 161° F for fifteen seconds.

In sterilizing foods for canning, the type of food and size of the containers must be taken into consideration in determining the proper time and temperature. The smaller the container, the faster the heat will be conducted through the food.

It is important to note once more that in order to destroy spore-forming bacilli completely, very high temperatures, often higher than 212° F are required for long time periods.

DESTRUCTION BY CHEMICALS

Bacteria can be destroyed by chemical agents. Those which kill all bacteria are called germicides or bactericides. Examples are phenol (carbolic acid), formaldehyde, iodine, chlorine, and others, such as the group of chemicals known as quarternary compounds. The effectiveness of the chemical bactericide depends on the concentration and the method with which it is used. If it is used to kill pathogenic organisms only, it is called a disinfectant. If a mild concentration is used on wounds to inhibit the growth of disease organisms, it is called an antiseptic. Some chemicals have been used in foods to inhibit the growth of spoilage bacteria, and these are called preservatives. Examples of these are sulphur dioxide, benzoate of soda, salt, sugar, and vinegar.

OTHER METHODS OF DESTRUCTION

When exposed to air and sunlight, bacteria are destroyed due to the combined effects of lack of moisture and food and exposure to the natural ultraviolet rays of the sun. Ultraviolet lamps are used for bactericidal purposes but their field is limited. Aeration is not used commercially as the sole means of sterilizing a product.

REFRIGERATION

Refrigeration of foods in refrigerators (32-45° F) does not kill bacteria. However, these temperatures do inhibit the growth of bacteria, both putrefactive and pathogenic, so that foods under proper refrigeration remain wholesome and free from disease for some time.

MICROBIOLOGY OF FOODS: BACTERIA AND OTHER MICROORGANISMS

Extremely low freezing temperatures for prolonged periods may result in the death of some bacteria, while others may survive. However, refrigeration or freezing should never be considered as a means of destroying bacteria; these methods merely retard bacterial growth.

VIRUSES

Viruses are minute organic forms which seem to be intermediate between living cells and organic compounds. They are smaller than bacteria, and are sometimes called filterable viruses because they are so small that they can pass through the tiny pores of a porcelain filter which retain bacteria. They cannot be seen through a microscope (magnification of 1500 x) but can be seen through an electron microscope (magnification of 1,000,000 x). Viruses cause poliomyelitis, smallpox, measles, mumps, encephalitis, influenza, and the common cold. Viruses, like bacteria are presumed to exist everywhere.

YEASTS

Yeasts are one-celled organisms which are larger than bacteria. They, too, are found everywhere, and require food, moisture, warmth, and air for proper growth. Unlike some bacteria which live without air, yeasts must have air in order to grow. They need sugar, but have the ability to change starch into sugar. When yeasts act on sugar, the formation of alcohol and carbon dioxide results. In the baking industry, yeast is used to *"raise dough"* through the production of carbon dioxide. The alcohol is driven off by the heat of the oven. In wine production, the carbon dioxide gas bubbles off, leaving the alcohol. The amount of alcohol produced by yeasts is limited to 18%, because yeasts are killed at this concentration of alcohol.

Yeasts reproduce by budding, which is similar to binary fission. Generally, the methods described for the destruction of bacteria will kill yeasts as well.

Yeasts are not generally considered to be pathogenic or harmful although a few of them do cause skin infections. Wild yeasts or those that get into a food by accident rather than by design of the food processor cause food spoilage and decomposition of starch and sugar, and therefore are undesirable.

MOLDS

Molds are multicellular (many-celled) microscopic plants which become visible to the naked eye when growing in sufficient quantity. Mold colonies have definite colors (white, black, green, etc.) They are larger than bacteria or yeasts. Some molds are pathogenic, causing such diseases as athletes' foot, ringworm, and other skin diseases. However, moldy foods usually do not cause illness. In fact, molds are encouraged to grow in certain cheeses to produce a characteristic flavor.

The structure of the mold consists of a root-like structure called the mycelium, a stem (ariel filament) called the hypha, and the spore sac, called the sporangium. All molds reproduce by means of spores. Molds are the lowest form of life that have these specialized reproductive cells.

Molds require moisture and air for growth and can grow on almost any organic matter, which does not necessarily have to be food. Molds do not require warmth, and grow very well in refrigerators. Neither do molds require much moisture, although the more moisture present, the better they multiply.

Methods of destruction for molds are similar to those required for bacteria. Heat, chemicals, and ultraviolet rays destroy mold spores as well as the molds. Refrigeration does not necessarily retard their growth.

Certain chemicals act as mold inhibitors. Calcium propionate (Mycoban) is one used in making bread. This chemical when used in the dough, retards the germination of mold spores, and bread so treated will remain mold-free for about five days.

One of the most beneficial molds is the Penicillium mold from which penicillin, an antibiotic, is extracted. The discovery, by Dr. Alexander Fleming, of the mold's antibiotic properties open up a whold field of research, and other antibiotic products from molds have been discovered.

CLASSIFICATION OF FOODBORNE DISEASE

Several terms are used to describe illness in which the causative agent is obtained by ingestion of food; the expression *"food poisoning"* is commonly employed to describe any of these. However, such usage is inaccurate and confusing.

Foodborne diseases caused by bacteria are divided into two classes. The first is called food intoxication (this is the real food poisoning) and designates illnesses due to toxins (poisons) secreted by bacteria growing in large numbers on the food prior to ingestion. In the second type of bacterial disease, called food infection, the symptoms are caused by the activity of large numbers of bacterial cells, having grown to some extent in the contaminated food, within the gastrointestinal system of the victim.

Other microbial contaminants of food, such as viruses, rickettsiae, and protozoa, can cause disease, as can other parasites. Chemical poisonings are characterized by a relatively sudden onset of symptoms, often in minutes. In addition, certain plants and animals contain chemical poisons, some of which produce illness within a short period after ingestion.

I. Food Intoxications
    A. Botulism
        1. Toxins are produced by growth of Clostridium botulinum in foods under anaerobic conditions. There are six major types of toxins: A, B, C, D, E and F. Types A, B, and E affect man. Antitoxins exist, although few hospitals routinely stock them.
        2. Symptoms: Toxin affects the central nervous system, producing difficulty in swallowing, double vision, and difficulty in speech and respiration, followed by death from paralysis of muscles of respiration.
        3. Onset of symtoms: 2 hours to 8 days, average 1 to 2 days.
        4. Inactivation of toxins: 15 minutes at 212° F.
        5. Foods usually involved: home-canned, low-acid vegetables. On rare occasions, commercially packed tuna, smoked fish, mushrooms, and vichysoisse.
    B. Staphylococcus Food Poisoning
        1. Toxin produced by coagulase positive Staphylococcus aureus.
        2. Symptoms: Nausea, vomiting, diarrhea, acute prostration, and abdominal cramps.
        3. Onset of symptoms: 1 to 6 hours, average 2-3 hours.
        4. Inactivation of toxin: Not inactivated by normal cooking times and temperatures.
        5. Foods usually involved: Ham, poultry, cream-filled bakery goods, protein salads.

II. Bacterial Food Infections
    A. Salmonellosis
        1. Salmonella typhimurium, Salmonella enteritidis, and others.
        2. Symptoms: Abdominal pain, diarrhea, chills, fever, frequent vomiting, and prostration.
        3. Onset of symptoms: 7 to 12 hours; average 12 to 24 hours.
        4. Inactivation: 165° F for period of cooking or heating.
        5. Foods usually involved: poultry, poultry products, inadequately cooked egg products, meats, and other foods.

B. Bacillary dysentery (Shigellosis)
   1. Various species of Shigella (Shigella dysenteriae, Shigella sonnei, and others.)
   2. Symptoms: Diarrhea, bloody stools, fever.
   3. Onset of symptoms: 1 to 7 days; average 2-3 days.
   4. Inactivation: 165° for period of cooking.
   5. Foods usually involved: Moist prepared foods and dairy products contaminated with excreta from carrier.
C. Streptococcal Infections (Scarlet fever or septic sore throat)
   1. Certain strains of beta-hemolytic streptococci
   2. Symptoms: Fever, sore throat.
   3. Onset of symptoms: 1 to 7 days; average 3 days.
   4. Inactivation: 165° F for period of cooking.
   5. Foods usually involved: Food contaminated with nasal or oral discharges from a case or carrier; raw milk from infected cows.
D. Enterococci (Fecal Streptococci)
   1. Various strains of Streptococcus fecalis.
   2. Symptoms: Nausea, sometimes vomiting and diarrhea.
   3. Onset of symptoms: 2 to 18 hours
   4. Inactivation: 165° F for period of cooking.
   5. Foods usually involved: Prepared food products contaminated with excreta.
E. Clostridium Perfringens
   1. Growth of Clostridium perfringens in food under anaerobic conditions.
   2. Symptoms: Acute abdominal pain and diarrhea, nausea, and rarely, vomiting.
   3. Onset of symptoms: 8 to 22 hours; average 8-12 hours.
   4. Inactivation: Variable, usually not inactivated by cooking temperatures.
   5. Foods usually involved: Poultry and meat products.

III. Viral Infections
   A. Infectious Hepatitis
      1. Virus of infectious hepatitis
      2. Symptoms: Fever, lack of appetite, malaise, fatigue, headache, nausea, chills, vomiting, jaundice may be present.
      3. Onset of symptoms: 14 to 35 days, average 25 days.
      4. Inactivation: not known.
      5. Foods usually involved: Shellfish (oyster, clams, mussels) taken from polluted waters and eaten raw; foods contaminated with excreta from an infected person.

IV. Parasitic Infections
   A. Trichinosis
      1. Trichinella spiralis.
      2. Symptoms: Nausea, vomiting, diarrhea (during digestion of trichinae); muscular pains, fever labored breathing, swelling of eyelids. Occassionally fatal.

3. Onset of symptoms: 2 to 28 days; average 9 days.
4. Inactivation: All parts of meat must reach 150° F to destroy cysts.
5. Foods usually involved: Raw or insufficiently cooked pork and pork products. Whale, seal, bear, and walrus meat have also been implicated.

B. Tapeworm (Taeniasis)
1. Taenia saginata (beef tapeworm); Taenia solium (pork tapeworm).
2. Symptoms: Beef tapeworm: abdominal pain, hungry feeling, vague discomfort. Pork tapeworm: varies from mild chronic digestive disorder to severe malaise.
3. Onset of symptoms: Several weeks.
4. Inactivation: All parts of the meat must reach 150° F.
5. Foods usually involved: Raw or insufficiently cooked beef or pork containing live larvae.

C. Fish Tapeworm Disease (Diphyllobothriasis)
1. Diphyllobothrium latum.
2. Symptoms: Anemia in heavy infections.
3. Onset of symptoms: 3 to 6 weeks.
4. Inactivation: All parts of fish meat must reach 150° F.
5. Foods usually involved: Raw or insufficiently cooked fish containing live larvae.

D. Amebic Dysentery
1. Entamoeba histolytica
2. Symptoms: Chronic diarrhea of varying severity or diarrhea alternating with constipation; occasionally fatal.
3. Onset of symptoms: 5 days to several months; average 3 to 4 weeks.
4. Inactivation: Cysts on vegetables destroyed by heating 30 minutes in water at 122° F.
5. Foods usually involved: Moist food contaminated with excreta from a carrier; contaminated water.

V. Poisonous Plants
A. Mushroom poisoning
1. Symptoms caused by phalloidine and other alkaloids of certain species of mushrooms.
2. Symptoms: Salivation: abdominal pain, intense thirst, nausea, vomiting, water stools, excessive perspiration, flow of tears; often fatal.
3. Onset of symptoms: 15 minutes to 15 hours.
4. Inactivation: Not inactivated by cooking.
5. Foods usually involved: Wild mushrooms, such as Amanita phalloides and Amanita muscaria, which are mistaken for edible mushrooms.

VI. Dangerous Chemicals
A. Antimony

1. Occurrence: Chipped grey enamelware in contact with acid foods and beverages.
2. Symptoms: Nausea, violent vomiting.
3. Onset of symptoms: 15 to 30 minutes.
4. Duration: Several hours.

B. Cadmium
1. Occurence: Cadmium used as plating, e.g., ice cube trays, dissolved in food or beverages.
2. Symptoms: Propulsive vomiting, nausea.
3. Onset of symptoms: 15 to 30 minutes.
4. Duration: Several hours.

C. Cyanide
1. Occurrence: Foods contaminated with silver polish containing cyanide.
2. Symptoms: Cyanosis (bluish discoloration of skin) mental confusion, glassy eyes, blue lips, often fatal.
3. Onset of symptoms: Almost instantaneous.

D. Lead
1. Occurrence: Food containers, solder containing more that 5% lead used on food equipment.
2. Symptoms: Blue line on gums, cramps in stomach, bowels, and legs, constipation, loss of appetite, headache, irritability.

E. Copper
1. Occurrence: Foods contaminated by copper salts (verdigris) on unclean copper utensils; beverages containing copper salts due to action of carbonation (carbon dioxide and water) on copper tubing.
2. Symptoms: Vomiting, abdominal pain, diarrhea.
3. Onset of symptoms: Usually immediate.

F. Zinc
1. Occurrence (rare): Acid foods cooked in galvanized (zinc-plated) utensils.
2. Symptoms: Dizziness, nausea, vomiting, tightness of throat.
3. Onset of symptoms: a few minutes to two hours.

G. Nitrites
1. Occurrence: Contamination of foods by nitrates, or nitrites used as a preservative in excess of 200 parts per million.
2. Symptoms: Cyanosis, shock, lowered blood pressure, methemoglobinemia (hemoglobin in blood combines with nitrites instead of oxygen producing internal asphyxiation.)
3. Onset of symptoms: 15 to 30 minutes.

H. Pesticides
1. Occurence: Foods accidentally contaminated with pesticides.

VII. Dangerous Animals
A. Shellfish
1. Occurrence: Shellfish grown in polluted waters, if eaten raw, can cause typhoid fever, cholera, and infectious hepatitis.

DISEASE PREVENTION IN RESTAURANTS

WHAT ARE THE MOST FAVORABLE CONDITIONS FOR THE GROWTH OF DISEASE GERMS?

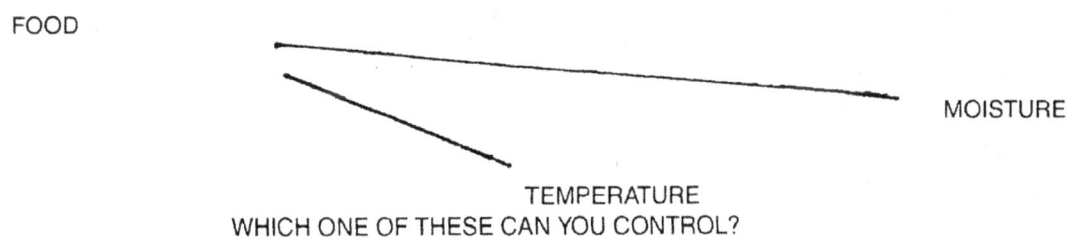

WHICH ONE OF THESE CAN YOU CONTROL?

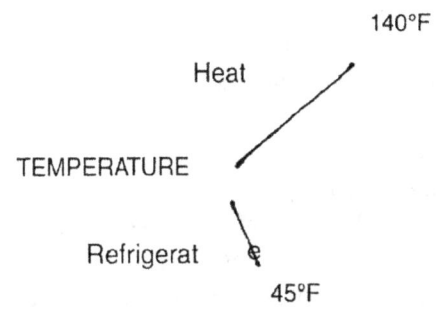

YOU CAN SPREAD DISEASE BY:

Carelessness
    Not washing hands before touching food, dishes, or utensils. Leaving food unprotected from dust, sneezes, rodents and insects. Using dirty equipment.
    Leaving food stand at room temperature.

Working when sick or with open sores
    Through food you infect.
    By direct contact with customers and fellow workers.
    By contaminating dishes and utensils.

YOU CAN GET DISEASE BY:
    Infection from a sick customer or fellow worker.
    Careless handling of soiled dishes.
    Eating infected food.
    Infection from rats, mice and insects.

FOOD PROTECTION

To Prevent Bacterial Food Poisoning and Infection
    Keep harmful bacteria out if possible.
    Keep them from growing if they do get in.
    How? By watching time and temperature, as well as cleanliness.

TIME
    Don't let food ready to serve stand longer than one hour at room temperature.

TEMPERATURE

Keep cold foods refrigerated at 45° F or lower until they are served.

Keep hot foods hot, above 140° F, until they are served.
WATCH THESE FOODS ESPECIALLY-BACTERIA LOVE THEM!
Cream filled or custard filled pastries, cakes and puddings.
Any dish made with cream sauce.
Meats, poultry and fish.
Dressing for poultry or meat.
Sandwiches, sandwich filling.

To Prevent Chemical Food Poisoning

Be sure all poisons are clearly labeled.
Never store poisons in food preparation areas.
Don't use insect sprays over or near food.
Don't keep any acid food or drink in a galvanized container.

SAFE STORAGE METHODS

Clean storage rooms, used for no other purpose.
All food stored at least six inches above floor.
Clean, neat refrigerator.
Food refrigerated in shallow containers, always covered.
Refrigerator shelves free of shelf-coverings.

SEVEN EASY RULES FOR SAFE FOOD

1. KEEP COLD FOODS COLD-HOT FOODS HOT. Don't let foods stand at room temperature.
2. KEEP HANDS CLEAN and touch food with hands as little as possible.
3. Don't let anyone with a skin infection or a cold handle food.
4. Keep kitchen, dining rooms and storage rooms free from rats, mice and insects.
5. Protect food from sneezes, customer handling, and dust.
6. Be sure poisons are well labeled and kept away from food preparation areas.
7. Wash dishes, glasses, silver and utensils by methods recommended by your health department.

Food Sanitation Guide

INTRODUCTION

Restaurants, hotel and catering services in the country and the city serve millions of meals daily. This places tremendous responsibility upon them in safeguarding public health by preparing and serving only wholesome foods.

There are a number of cardinal principles which must be observed in preparing and serving wholesome foods. The bacterial contamination of these foods can be kept at a minimum if these principles are followed.

The food-handler must always be aware that he may contaminate the product by poor personal hygiene and work habits. He must always keep his person clean and work tools in a clean and sanitary condition.

Food must be stored in such a manner as to protect it from contamination. Unfortunately unless the food is sterilized, which is rarely practical, the presence of some bacteria is unavoidable. In order to keep their growth to a minimum, proper time and temperature control methods must be practiced.

Special care must be taken in the handling of foods which are to be served without further heat treatment. Ready-to-eat foods must not be subjected to contamination by coming into contact with unprocessed or partially processed foodstuffs or unsanitized work surfaces and implements.

Wholesome foods cannot be prepared in a dirty plant. The importance of good housekeeping cannot be minimized as a factor in the production of wholesome foods.

These general principles are more fully developed in the guide that follows.

I. Food Storage

The recommendations and prohibitions made below, if followed, will result in a wholesome and bacterialogically sound food product.

    A. Dry Storage Foods
1. Dry stored foods are to be protected against contamination by insects, rodents, dust and other types of dirt.
2. All food storage containers should be properly labeled.

    B. Cold Storage
1. Frozen foods
(a) During storage frozen foods are to be completely frozen until ready for use. ($0°$ F)
(b) The freezer should be equipped with a thermometer so freezer temperatures can be determined without entering the holding box.
(c) Foods are to be stored in an orderly manner to assure cold air circulation and are not to be stored directly on the floor.

    C. Chilled Foods
1. Chilled foods should be kept at 45oF or less at all times. This may be done by the use of a walk-in refrigerator, reach-in refrigerator, refrigerated show cases, refrigerator counter and refrigerated tables, etc.
2. Refrigerators should be supplied with appropriate thermometers.
3. Containers holding foods should not be stored so that the bottom surface of the container rests on the surface of the food product in the container below it.
4. Cooked foods should be stored so that they do not become contaminated by raw foods.
5. All foodstuffs should be stored in such a manner as to protect them from contamination.

    D. Storage of Hot Foods

Foods to be served hot soon after cooking should not at any time be allowed to drop below an internal temperature of $14°$ F. If food is not to be served immediately upon completion of the cooking, it may be kept at temperatures in excess of $14°$ F by the use of warming cabinets, steamtables, chafing dishes or any other devices suitable for these purposes. Hot perishable foods are not to be kept at room temperature when the internal and surface temperature of the food falls below $140°$ F. Rare roast beef can be an exception to this. (See handling of rare roast beef, Pages 7-9)

II. Cleaning and Sanitization of Equipment and Kitchen Utensils

Equipment, utensils and work surfaces which come in contact with food should be thoroughly cleaned and sanitized before and after food preparation.

    A. Methods of Cleaning and Sanitizing

Prior to washing, manually remove all adhering food particles. Then wash, using a suitable soap or detergent, and hot water liberally applied by manual or mechanical means. After rinsing and removing all visible dirt and grease, sanitize using one of the following methods:

1. Heat Sanitization

(a) Clean hot water, $170°$ F or more, applied to all surfaces of the equipment or utensils for at least 30 seconds.

2. Chemical Sanitization
   (a) Apply a commercial preparation (Sodium Hypochlorite type) being sure to follow label directions.
   (b) If a commercial product is not available or desired, a suitable solution may be prepared by mixing 1/2 ounce of household bleach, (5.25% Sodium Hypochlorite) in one gallon of lukewarm water (do not use hot water). Flood the surfaces of the equipment and utensils with this solution for at least one minute. Do not rinse or wipe after this operation.
   If necessary to dry, air dry. Do not use a solution which is more than two hours old. If more solution is required, prepare a fresh supply.

III. Principles of Food Preparation and Services

During food preparation, improper techniques may contaminate the product with disease-causing organisms. It is for this purpose that sanitary procedures must be observed. Listed below are some principles which should be followed.

A. Food that is to be served cold should be kept cold ($45°$ F or less) through all stages of storage, processing, and serving. Thawing of frozen foods should be accomplished in such a manner so as to keep the surface and internal temperatures of the product $45°$ F or less at all times. If frozen food is to be thawed in water, running cold water is to be used.

B. Foods to be served hot are to be kept so that the internal and surface temperatures do not fall below $140°$ F. (See handling of rare roast beef - Pages 7-9). Care must be taken in the cooling of hot foods so they do not become contaminated by dust, contact with work clothes, human contact, etc. Cooling should be accomplished as quickly as possible by the use of fans, refrigeration, etc. To determine the temperature of foods, a food thermometer is to be used. (Hands are not to be used).

C. Partially processed and leftover foods are to be refrigerated at $45°$ F. or below. Just prior to service they are to be removed from the refrigerator and heated rapidly to serving temperatures so that the internal temperatures are not less than $140°$ F.

D. The holding of perishable foods between the temperatures of $140°$ and $45°$ F is to be kept at a minimum.

E. Contact of ready-to-eat foods with bare hands should be kept at an irreducible minimum and utensils should be used whenever possible.

F. Ready-to-eat foods should not be contaminated by coming in contact with work surfaces, equipment, utensils or hands previously in contact with raw foods until such surfaces, etc. have been cleaned and sanitized.

G. Do not place packing cases and cans on food work surfaces.

H. When necessary to taste foods during processing, a clean sanitized utensil should be used. When tasting again, either re-clean and re-sanitize utensil, or use another sanitized utensil.

I. Foods are to be cooked and processed as close to the time of service as possible.

J. Menu planning should be such as to prevent excessive leftovers, and leftovers are not to be pooled with fresh foods during storage.

IV. Transportation of Foods

In some food operations, it is necessary to transport food from a central kitchen (commissary) to an establishment where it is finally served. The food transported can be in a ready-to-eat state or a pre-cooked stage, which is finally processed at the place of service. The following practices should be observed to see that contamination is not introduced or possible previous bacterial contamination not afforded means for extensive multiplication during this period.

1. Transporting containers and vehicles should be clean and of sanitary design to facilitate cleaning.
2. Transporting containers and vehicles should have acceptable refrigerating and/or heating facilities for maintaining food at cold (45° F or below) or hot (above 140°) temperatures while in transit.
3. Food stored in transporting containers and vehicles should be protected from contamination.
4. A minimum amount of time is to be taken for the loading and unloading of foods from transporting vehicles so foods will not be exposed to adverse temperatures and conditions.

V. Food Processing Techniques Relative to Specific Types of Service
    A. Displayed Food (Buffet, Smorgasbord, etc.)

1. Hot foods are to be kept at or above 140° F on the display table by use of chafing dishes, steam tables or other suitable methods.
2. Cold foods are to be at temperatures 45° F. or less before being displayed and not to be exposed at room temperature for more than one hour unless some means is employed, (ice, mechanical refrigeration, etc.) to keep cold foods at or less than 45° F.
3. All foods displayed and, therefore, subject to contamination must be discarded at the conclusion of the buffet service.

    B. Protein Type Salads (Tuna, Ham, Shrimp, Egg, Chicken, Lobster, etc.)

These salads are always served cold and, therefore, all salad ingredients except the seasoning and spices are to be chilled to 45° F or less before use. Celery, which is almost always a component of these salads, should be treated so as to minimize its bacterial content by the immersing of the chopped celery in boiling water, using a hand strainer or colander for 30 seconds and then chilling immediately by holding under running cold tap water.

Before the mixing operation, the previously washed can opener, and tops of cans and jars holding salad ingredients should be wiped with a clean cloth containing sanitizing solution. The salad ingredients should be mixed with clean, sanitizing equipment, (sanitary type masher, sanitary mixing bowl, stainless steel long handled spon or fork, mechanical tumbler type mixer, etc.). There should be an absolute minimum of bare hand contact with the equipment and ingredients. The mixing operation is to be completed as quickly as possible and the finished salad immediately served or refrigerated.

    C. Additional Instructions Relative to Specific Salads

1. Shrimp and Lobster Salad
   Immerse shrimp, or lobster meat in boiling water for 30 seconds and then chill to 45° F or less before adding to salad. Fast chilling can be accomplished by placing the meat in shallow pans in the freezer or refrigerator or on top of cracked ice.
2. Egg Salad
   After removing shell, use a hand strainer or colander to immerse hard-boiled eggs in boiling water for 30 seconds and then chill to 45° F or less before adding to salad. Chill the eggs by refrigerating or by placing strainer containing them under running cold tap water.
3. Chicken and/or Turkey Salad
   After removal from bones, immerse chicken or turkey meat in boiling water or boiling stock for 30 seconds and then chill to 45° F. before adding to salad. Fast chilling can be accomplished by placing the meat in shallow pans in the freezer, refrigerator or on cracked ice.
4. Ham Salad
   Immerse diced ham in boiling water or boiling stock for 30 seconds and then chill to 45° F. or less before adding to salad. Fast chilling can be accomplished by the same method used for chicken and shrimp.

D. Hot Meats and Poultry Served from Steamtables or Other Suitable Warming Devices
1. Schedule the cooking of meats so they will be completed as close as possible to desired time of service.
2. Upon removal from the oven or stove, cooked meats are to be kept at an internal temperature of 140° F or higher in a steamtable or other suitable device.
3. Maintain the water in the steamtable at a temperature in excess of 180° F. The water must be brought to this temperature before any foods are placed therein. Water in the steamtable shall be kept at a steamtable depth so as to be in contact with the bottom and upper portions of the sides of the food container.
4. Refrigerated ready-to-eat cooked meats, especially leftovers, gravies and stocks, are to be heated rapidly to an internal temperatures of 165° F or higher before being placed in the steamtable or warming device. Hot stock or meat gravies may be used to reheat meats. Steamtables or other warming devices should never be used to heat up cold meats.
5. Cautions noted previously relative to hand contact, care of equipment storage, and menu planning should also be followed.

E. Roast Beef

   Because of consumer preference, roast beef is often served at an internal temperature of less than 140° F. Continuous warming and heating of this product, as for example on a steamtable, may not be practical as it causes the meat to become well done and thus less desirable to some consumers. It is, therefore, realized that instructions relative to maintenance of interior temperatures of meat cannot always be applied to this product. It is essential, therefore, that Roast Beef be cooked as close to time of service as possible. Great care must be taken to prevent contamination. At large banquets this roast is sometimes stored or "rested" for excessive lengths of time, during which bacterial growth can occur.

1. Bone in Standing Rib Roast

    There are a number of methods to be used in the processing of this type of roast beef, which will help minimize bacterial contamination and growth.

    (a) Method No. 1

    The roast is boned and trimmed prior to cooking. Slicing is accomplished after cooking and immediately prior to serving. After removal from the oven, the surface temperature should be in excess of $140°$ F. This method minimizes the amount of handling after the cooking operations.

    (b) Method No. 2

    After cooking and storage the roast is boned, trimmed (all surfaces) and sliced immediately prior to service. This method removes almost all surface contamination.

    (c) Method No. 3

    The surface of the raw roast beef is coated with a concentration of coarse salt. The beef is cooked and stored with this coating intact and it is not removed until just prior to service, at which time, boning and trimming and slicing takes place. The salinity on the surface of the meat inhibits the bacterial growth. It has been found that after removal of the salt coating platibility of the meat is not impaired as there is practically no penetration of the salt into the edible portion of the meat.

2. Boneless Tied Roast Beef

    This type of roast beef is commonly machine sliced and used on sandwiches and platters. As stated above this type of roast beef is often desired rate where high internal temperatures cannot be applied.

    Menu planning should be such that the roast beef should be removed from the oven as close to the service time as possible.

    After removing a large roast beef from the oven, it should be cut into smaller pieces, each not to exceed 6 pounds. The surface temperature of the meat should not fall below $140°$., at which time the roast can be sliced for immediate service and placed in the refrigerator, warming oven or steamtable. The refrigerator temperature should be below $45°$ F and steamtable temperature in excess of $140°$ F.

    It is suggested that only one piece of roast be kept for immediate service and the other pieces be stored in the refrigerator or warming device. At the end of the day any piece of roast beef which has been partially used should be considered as a leftover. This piece of meat must be refrigerated overnight, and before being reused it is to be heated to an internal temperature in excess of $165°$ F. It is realized that after cooking at these temperatures, this product cannot be served again as rare roast beef.

The slicing machine used for this product should be dissassembled and cleaned at the end of the day's work, and left disassembled. Before beginning slicing operations the next day, it is to be sanitized and reassembled.

    3. Steamship (Steamer) Beef Roasts

This type of roast consists of the whole beef round (top and bottom) usually served rare and stored at inadequate temperatures (less that $140°$). This product is almost always hand carved. (The term hand carved is used to denote that it is not machine sliced). There is no need for hand contact inasmuch as this meat is sliced with the use of a chef's knife and fork and transferred to the sandwich or platter using these utensils. Since the normal means to prevent contamination cannot be excercised, it is mandatory that only properly sanitized equipment be used and the food-handler exert particular care not to contaminate the product. As stated above in paragraph 2, any unused portion of this roast should be refrigerated, and before being served again cooked to an internal temperature of $165°$ F. It is again realized that after recooking at this temperature this product cannot be served as rare roast beef.

F. Rare Steaks

If these are not cooked immediately prior to service, it is sometimes the practice to singe the outer surface of the meat, and then store it at room temperature until the time of service. It is cooked by broiling and served immediately.

For this type of meat service, it is important that the storage period is not over one hour, the meat does not come in contact with contaminated work surfaces or hands and the meat is subjected to sufficient surface terminal heat treatment just before serving.

G. Pre-cooked Hamburger Patties

It has become a practice in some restaurants to pre-cook hamburger patties, and store them in a warmer or above the stove or grill until needed for service. In most cases the temperatures and lengths of time the meat is kept can be such as to allow the growth of pathogenic organisms.

If this type of food preparation is practiced, extreme care should be taken to see that this product is not stored for more than one hour, the food is not contaminated by unclean hands or work surfaces, and it receives a thorough heat treatment (exceeding $16°$ F) just prior to its consumption.

H. Pre-cooked Chicken - (Barbecued Style)

This product, a whole eviscerated chicken of 2-3 pounds, is usually cooked in a rotisserie-type radiant heating device and stored for varying lengths of time and temperature. Again this type of food storage is advantageous for the growth of food poisoning organisms.

Precautions to be followed with this product are: all parts of the poultry are to be thoroughly and completely cooked (over $165°$ F); it is to be handled and stored so that it will not come in contact with contaminated hands or work surfaces; and it shall not be kept at temperatures between 45° F and 14° F for more than one hour anytime prior to consumption.

I. Poultry Stuffing

Often times adequate internal temperatures are not obtained in the cooking of stuffed poultry. The temperature of the stuffing is such as to incubate rather than destroy bacteria. It is therefore advisable to cook the stuffing separately from the poultry. When this is done adequate temperatures (165° F) are reached in both the stuffing and poultry. Thereafter the stuffing should be handled and/or stored in a manner similar to that noted previously for perishable protein foods.

J. Custard-Filled Baked Goods

The problems with custard fillings arise after completion of the cooking operation during the cooling and handling period. The following recommendations are made:

1. Utensils and receptacles must be sanitized as previously noted.
2. The finished custard should be transferred to shallow stainless steel or aluminum trays to facilitate rapid cooling. It is important at this point not to contaminate the product with the foodhandler's hands or clothing.
3. A long-bladed flexible spatula of sanitary construction should be used to scrape the residue from the cooking receptacle.
4. The finished product should be refrigerated as quickly as possible and at no time should the product be exposed to room temperature for more than one hour.
5. The shallow pans of custard should be covered with wax or other clean paper while cooling and while being stored in the refrigerator.
6. Jelly-filling machines of sanitary design should be used. Multiple use pastry bags, after washing, are to be boiled or sanitized before use. A single service pastry bag can be fashioned out of wax or parchment paper. A desire method of filling eclair shells, cream puffs and similar type products is to cut the shell in half and apply the filling with a properly sanitized stainless steel spatula. This is the only method to be used in the production of napoleans.
7. Butter cream which is to be used as an ingredient of custard should be handled with the same precautions as actual custard.
8. The finished product, immediately after completion, must be kept under refrigeration (45° F or less) at all times until consumed. Commercial fillings, bavarian creams, etc., are often used instead of true custard. They are used, as per label directions, and are sometimes used with the addition of eggs, cream, butter cream, etc., depending on the recipe of the individual food processor. The same care, relative to the boiling and refrigeration of all ingredients, should be taken in the manufacture of these products as is observed with true custard.

K. Deviled Eggs

It has been the experience of the Food Processing Control Unit that this product is needlessly contaminated by poor handling techniques. The following is suggested to minimize contamination.

1. This product is to be prepared as close to service as possible.
2. After the shell is removed from the egg, the peeled egg is to be placed in a strainer or colander and then in boiling water for not less than 30 seconds and then immediately plgced in running cold water and chilled to 45° F or less.
3. At this point, when it is unavoidable that the bare hands be used, it is mandatory that the food handler wash his hands thoroughly with a germicidal soap before proceeding with the process.
4. Whenever possible remove the yolk of the egg with a sanitized utensil, and when the yolk is mashed and mixed with seasonings, a sanitized utensi' is also to be used.
5. In extruding the mashed yolk, a single service pastry bag is recommended. If a multiple use bag is desired it is to be sanitized by heat or chemical treatment prior to use.
6. If the finished product is not used immediately, it is to be refrigerated at 45° F or less until served.

L. Fresh Pork Products

Though it has been previously mentioned that meats are to be cooked to proper internal temperatures, it is felt that an additional warning be given concerning fresh pork products. Government inspection of fresh pork is not a guarantee against trichina contamination of this product. The trichina are not readily detectable except by microscopic examination and then only if an infested area is examined. It is therefore mandatory that fresh pork products be cooked to an internal temperature of at least 150° F.

M. Chopped Liver

This perishable, popular product is ordinarily literally manhandled in processing. Inasmuch as most of the handling takes place after cooking and the product is served without further heat treatment extra precautions must be taken to minimize hand contact.

Equipment must be cleaned and sanitized before use. It is best to clean, sanitize, and assemble equipment immediately prior to use. Ingredients should not be touched with bare hands after cooking. Cooked liver is to be handled with sanitized equipment only. Hard boiled eggs, after shells are removed, are to be placed in a colander or strainer and immersed in boiling water for 30 seconds and then placed in running cold water and chilled to 45°F or less. The peeled eggs are then to be handled by implements only. After mixing, the finished chopped liver is to be placed in stainless steel serving containers or molds without use of bare hands. If hand molding is required for a decorative display this is to be done immediately prior to service.

VI. Plant Sanitation and Maintenance

The unclean and defective condition of the physical plant, walls, floors, ceilings, doors, windows, etc., can adversely affect the final product from a bacterial standpoint. Care should be taken to see that they are clean and maintained in such a manner as to facilitate proper plant sanitation. It is known that bacterial organisms will establish themselves on encrusted foods such as is found on walls, light switches, room and refrigerator door handles, and other surfaces touched by food-handlers. Improper wall, window and door maintenance, ineffective cleaning and poor garbage disposal methods can also lead to insect and rodent infestations. These well known vectors of disease organisms can introduce food poisoning bacteria to foodstuffs in the establishment. (When necessary acceptable insecticides and rodenticides can be used to prevent or exterminate an infestation of these pests. Care should be observed to see they do not come in contact with foodstuffs.)

Adequate amounts of hot and cold running water should be supplied at properly maintained fixtures, strategically placed in parts of the plant, i.e., toilets, food processing areas, utensil cleaning areas, etc. Such fixtures should also be supplied with detergents, bactericides, and single service hand towels.

Equipment should be of sanitary design and maintained in a sanitary condition, cleaned after use and sanitized before use. Open seams and worn or defective surfaces which allow food particles to accumulate and prevent proper cleaning should be repaired forthwith.

Self-inspection and cleaning schedules should be devised for all areas of the plant and equipment. At routine periods all areas should be inspected to detail and findings noted on a form devised for this purpose. Follow-up on findings should be made as soon as feasible.

Cleaning and maintenance should follow every major production period. If production is continuous for a 12 or 18 hour period, "down" periods should be incorporated in the work schedule to allow for this sanitation program.

VII. Non-Commercial Food Operations

This guide is primarily for the use of the sanitarian and the operators of commercial food-processing establishments. In a city of this size, many large meals and buffets are prepared and served by private and volunteer organizations. These include church and synogogue socials, local charity and fund raising affairs, fraternal organizations, etc.

These types of affairs often lead to food-borne illnesses when proper precautions are not taken. It is therefore important that the recommendations contained herein also be practiced by these large non-commercial feeding operations.

VIII. Assistance to Food Processors

Commercial and non-commercial food operations are urged to use the expertise of this department by calling upon us to discuss and analyze problems occuring in their food handling programs.

SALAD PREPARATION GUIDE

1. Refrigerate all salad ingredients except seasoning and spices overnight or chill to 45° F or lower before use.
2. Purchase a sanitizing solution or prepare one by mixing one or two ounces of bleach to a gallon of cold water. This solution is effective for approximately two hours. Prepare a fresh solution if further sanitization is needed.
3. Clean work surfaces, equipment and utensils (pots, pans, spoons, spatulas, etc.) with soap and hot water, rinse with clean water, and then give a final rinse with sanitizing solution. Stainless steel utensils and equipment are preferred in preparation of these foods.
4. Clean hands, fingernails, and arms thoroughly with ger-micidal soap and hot water and dry with single use paper towels.
5. Individuals preparing salads are not to perform other tasks while engaged in salad preparation.
6. Clean and sanitize tops of cans and jars before openings. Do not use fingers to pry off can lids or drain off liquid contents.
7. Place diced celery, including pre-cut packaged celery in a strainer and immerse in boiling water for 30 seconds; then chill to 45° F or less.
8. Use clean sanitized utensils in mixing and handling of foods. Avoid hand contact with foods.
9. Refrigerate final salad product immediately in shallow pans.
10. Salads placed in bain-marie cold plates should have a minimum internal temperature of 45° F.
11. Do not fill trays above spill line.

BASIC FUNDAMENTALS OF INSECT AND RODENT CONTROL

CONTENTS

	Page
1. BRIEF HISTORY	1
2. COCKROACHES	1
3. FLIES	3
4. ANTS	3
5. TERMITES	3
6. BEDBUGS	5
7. LICE	6
8. RODENTS	7

BASIC FUNDAMENTALS OF INSECT AND RODENT CONTROL

PURPOSE: Prevent entry, reduce the threat of infection and disease and to provide a sanitary environment.

EQUIPMENT:

    Knowledge of life cycle, habitation and signs of infestations
    Good housekeeping
    Denial of entry and access to food
    Chemical insecticides guided by the Environmental Protection Agency (EPA)

SAFETY PRECAUTIONS:

1. Be aware: Insects and rodents are not just nuisance to man, they are regarded as health hazards. Insects carry disease and bacteria and rodents carry fleas that transmit Typhus and Bubonic Plague.

2. Report signs of insects or rodents to Sanitary Engineering Branch.

3. Be safety conscious of chemical insecticides. Use poisons and insecticides under supervision only, and as directed by EPA.

4. Keep chemical poisons away from food, covered, clearly labeled and stored in locked cabinets.

5. Never use insecticides before reading label.

6. Make sure insecticide is registered by the U.S.D.A. before purchasing.

1. **BRIEF HISTORY:**

There are over 500,000 species of insects but only 1% are of any real concern to man. This 1% causes 200 different types of diseases. Their sizes vary from $1/16$ of an inch to 7 inches. Among the insects causing the most disease and destruction are: cock-roaches, flies, mosquitoes, ants, bed bugs, moths, lice, termites and fleas.

2. **COCKROACHES:**

Cockroaches are pale tan, mahogany or black in color with long slender antennae.

The 4 types of roaches most commonly found in institutions are:

    1. The German roach—Blatella Germanica—the craton bug.
    2. Brown-banded roach—Supella Supelectillium.
    3. Oriental roach—Blatella Orientalis—Shad roach.
    4. American Roach—Periplanetta Americana—The Bombay Canary.

The Cockroach is an ancient creature that has adapted itself to the abode of man and can be the most troublesome insect in an institution. The offensive secretions of these insects, and their loathsome habit of crawling on filth, then onto dishes and food; has made them among the most despised of vermin. They are also potential vectors of disease.

Control measures include complete cleanliness and removal or denial of access of food, storing foods properly in closed containers and use of insecticides. Some authorities state that the powder insecticide is the most effective control for roaches. However, roaches have built up a resistance to insecticides.

REPORTS OF VIRGINIA POLYTECHNICAL INSTITUTE (AS OF DECEMBER 1960) FOR RESISTANT COCKROACHES.

Today more than ever in the history of the world, man is becoming acutely aware of the stability of insect life, for man with all of his knowledge and wisdom, his scientific research, and modern laboratories realizes that he is dealing with nature in all of its mystic powers. No matter what he develops in the way of control methods, nature has always had the ability to overthrow its potentialities.

Almost every person today is confronted with some insect problem, whether it be roaches, flies, fleas, ticks or moths. As he investigates the market for materials to combat these insects, he finds that he gets very little results and because of this, soon realizes that something strange is going on in the insect world.

What is happening? This is the problem that our scientists are trying to solve today, the question of just how and why these insects are able to build up immunity against such powerful chemicals compounded out of hydrocarbons and phosphates.

In 1947, studies were begun at V.P.I. by Dr. J. M. Grayson, who was joined in 1957, by Dr. D. G. Cochron using a selection of populations of German roaches for resistance to various insecticides. There are now six or seven different projects being carried out in the insecticide resistance areas.

For the last 12 to 14 years the standard control procedure for German roaches has been 2% solution of Chlordane. It is now known that Chlordane resistance is common in all parts of the country, where this has happened the insecticide Diazinon is recommended, however, there has been reports that resistance to Diazinon is also developing.

The problem of stability or how long will resistance hold up if the insects are no longer exposed to the insecticides, is one which these scientists have been trying to determine. There had not been enough time to determine the longevity of the phosphate insecticides; however, they do have sufficient information concerning the hydrocarbon insecticides such as Chlordane, D.D.T., Lindane. They have found that resistance to D.D.T. is lost quite rapidly, and when the insects are re-exposed, resistance develops very slowly; however, with Chlordane and Lindane, resistance lasts for a considerably longer time. With resistance of 20% after 25 generations of insects that are not exposed to any chemicals and when re-exposed, these insects build resistance in two generations. So, we find that the problem of resistance to insecticides by the German Roach is one which warrants continuing studies.

Dr. Grayson carried out extensive studies, testing new materials and formulating new materials against resistant roaches. The following are a few of the chemicals tested and their results:

1. The compound Chemagro 29493 or Baytex as it is called gave good results in a 1% emulsion form.

2. The results in oil were not as good.

3. The material Butonate at the .8% level in oil

INSECT AND RODENT CONTROL

was not very promising; however, at a higher percentage it may do a better job.

4. The material D.D.V.P. did not hold up over a 60-day period in a 2% solution with Dieldrin. This material however, at a .5% might prove effective and this percentage has recently been approved by the pesticide regulation section of the U.S.D.A. for limited use by P.C.O. only. This action is based upon the fact that D.D.V.P. in the vapor form is not as hazardous as previously thought. It is still, however, a dangerous material, and should be used with a great deal of care.

5. The material, Hercules 7522C, which is a carbonate material was *not* effective in these tests.

6. Malathion SF60, which is a formulation of Malathion designed to give longer residual action was proven not to be good, however, it did work in some areas.

7. The compound, Monsanto CP 11223 is an excellent roach control material; however, because of its limitations as far as other insects are concerned the manufacturer feels that the roach market is not sufficient enough to warrant the manufacturing of this material. We are given to think that this material will not be pursued further.

8. The compound Diazinon in a 5% solution was found to be the standard in these tests and gave good results.

3. FLIES:

A winged insect that emerges from larvae—or maggots, as they are most commonly called and feed on the materials of their surroundings. There are several species:

1. House Fly—Musca Domesticus.
2. Blow—Phornia Regina.
3. Bottle—Family Calliphoridae.
4. Fruit—Drosophila.
5. The Lesser House Fly—Eannia Canicularis.

The House fly, however, out numbers the other species listed, therefore, the following discussion will pertain to the House fly. It lays its eggs in human and animal excrement. Under favorable (warm) weather conditions, the larvae to adult stage takes 8 to 12 days. Aside from being one of the most annoying insects, it spreads disease.

The primary control measure against flies must be taken at its breeding place. Complete cleanliness and removal of food are the best control against flies. Insecticides are used under supervision only and as directed by EPA.

4. ANTS:

Any of an order of Hymenoptera which includes the bee, the wasp and other related forms that often associate in large colonies with complex social organization. Ants are just nuisance, they have not been implicated as disease spreader. However, they must be controlled in buildings, because of their ability to destroy food and because they are unwelcomed guests. Good sanitation inside buildings and on surrounding grounds is essential.

5. TERMITES:

Any of numerous pale-colored soft-bodied social insects (order of Isoptera) that live in colonies consisting of winged sexual forms, wingless sterile workers and often soldiers. They feed on wood. They have an appearance very *similar* to ants.

Signs of infestation: Clay or dirt packed on basement floor joist (forms the termite tunnels) or pitting of the floor joist.

Call the Sanitary Engineering Branch if any of

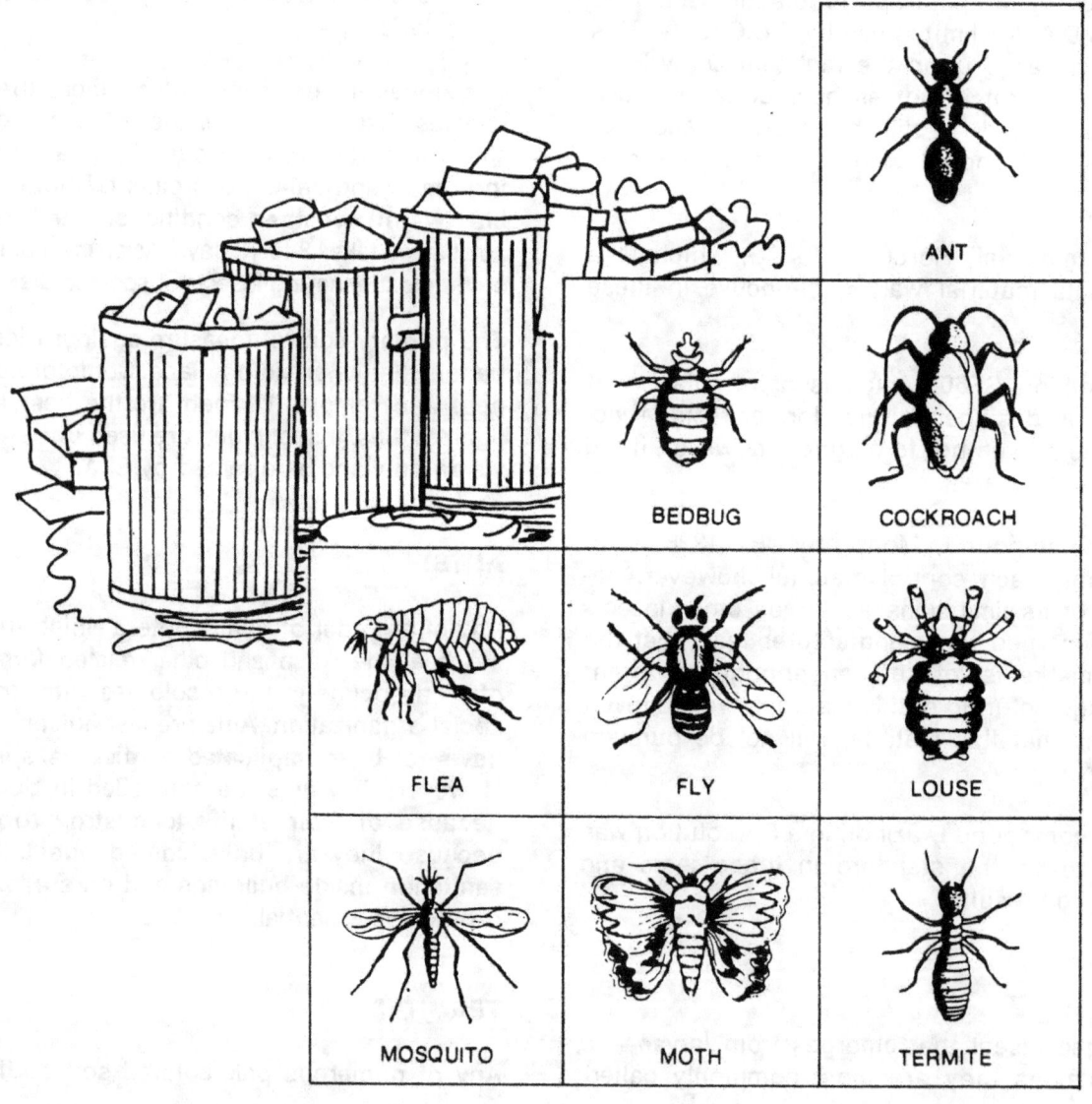

INSECT AND RODENT CONTROL

these signs are observed—only professional control measures are effective.

The following are some suggestions that will keep *new* buildings free from these subterranean insects for many years:

1. Site Sanitation: All tree stumps, roots and surplus wood should be removed from the site before construction is started. All surplus wood and grade stakes should be removed as soon as construction is finished. When these items are left in the soil, they become food to establish colonies in the soil.

2. Foundation Structure: It is important to make the foundation impervious to termite attack. Poured reinforced concrete with expansion joints properly filled, makes the best resistant contruction. All wood work resting on, not through the foundation, should be properly treated to protect it from damage. A popular method is the use of Pentachlorophenol, a wood preservative, in oil, soaked into the wood. This type of material after it is dried, permits painting. It is generally used at 5% solution in oil.

3. Ventilation and Drainage: In construction where there are crawl areas, cross ventilation is highly desirable to control the moisture conductive to termite existence. The amount of ventilators needed depends on the area, the humidity and air currents. This is also true of the front steps adjoining the building.

4. Drainage: The soil adjacent to the building should be so graded as to permit the water to drain away from the structure. Proper guttering, draining well away from the corners are vital. All areas under the building must be properly drained.

5. Clearance Beneath the Building: In order to make periodic inspections under the building, a clearance of 18" from the joist to the ground is desirable to facilitate the inspection.

6. Skirting: When used, a clearance of 3 to 6" between it and the ground should be allowed. If this is filled in during the winter, it should be reopened in the spring.

7. Miscellaneous Appendaged: Porches, steps, terraces and platforms should be treated and installed in such a way as to prevent soil from coming into contact with them. Sleepers and studs should not be imbedded in concrete. Plumbing should be installed clear of the ground and not supported by wooden or any other braces that come in contact with the soil. This would permit termites to build tubes that would reach the floor joists. All areas where pipes or conduits enter into the floor or wall from below ground, including expansion joints, should be thoroughly filled with old style roofing pitch.

8. Chemical Soil Barriers: Pretreatment to the soil with residual insecticides should be added to the soil during construction at the rate of 1 gallon of 1% Chlordane emulsion to 10 square feet of flat ground or 2 gallons per linear foot of trenching and footing and wall void treatment.

6. BEDBUGS:

A wingless blood sucking bug—reddish brown in color (Cimex Lectularius). Found in bedding, cracks, crevices of walls and ground baseboards.

Their presence are detected by their odor, blood stains and excretory spots. General cleanliness is the first line of defense.

INSECT AND RODENT CONTROL

7. LICE:

The orders, Anoplura and Mallophaga are known collectively as lice. All known numbers of both orders are wingless parasites of warm blooded animals but the members of the two orders differ considerable in the structure and feeding habits. The order Anoplura is made up of two members which have sucking mouthparts and which feed upon blood. The members of the order Mallophaga have chewing mouthparts and feed on skin scales and secretions.

Because all the lice are parasitic and spend virtually all their lifetime on the host, the pest control operator is seldom directly involved in the actual process of louse control. In practically every situation encountered, successful louse control involves direct treatment to the host animal. The responsibility for such treatments belong to physicians and veterinarians.

However, special precautionary measures should be observed as specified when entering the infected area or when handling the belongings of an infested person (observe isolation precaution measures).

Sucking Lice, Order Anoplura: This order is a rather small one, containing approximately 500 species, two of which are parasites of man. The antennae have no more than five segments, the head is narrower than the thorax, and the thoracic segments are fused and cannot be moved independently from the abdomen. In practically all species in which the life history had been studied, the eggs, young and adults are all found on the host. Only mammals are parasitized by this order. The adult female attaches its eggs to the hair of the host, the young and the adults suck blood from the host.

Human Louse Pediculus Humanus SSP. Family: Pediculidae: This species has been the subject of spirited controversy among experts on the classification of this group. Biologically, there are two rather distinct patterns of behavior within the species and many authorities feel that this is actually a complex of two species. These two entities will be considered subspecies in this discussion.

The human louse is important from the standpoint of its activities as a parasite but is even more detrimental to human welfare as a means of spreading the casual organisms of typhus and relapsing fever. Circumstances that cause large numbers of people to be crowded together under unsanitary conditions are most favorable to the rapid development of large louse populations and this fact accounts for the ever present danger of typhus outbreaks in such situations.

Body Louse: Pediculus Humanus Humanus: This is the larger of the two subspecies involved, being generally more than three millimeters long and the integument is relatively soft.

Probably the most important characteristic which differs in the subspecies, is the tendency of the boy louse to remain on the body of the host only during the process of actual feeding. When no feeding, the body louse conceals itself in the clothing of the host. Associated with this behavior is the habit of placing the eggs on the fibers of the garments of the host instead of attaching them directly to the body hair.

This type of egg placement is probably a unique habit which does not occur in other sucking lice.

Since treatment of the clothing of people in-

INSECT AND RODENT CONTROL

fested with body lice is an important part of any control measure, the PCO may often play an important part in louse control program. Infested clothing can be sprayed with 0.25% Lindane, 4% Malathion dust.

Head Louse: Pediculus Humanus Capitus: This typical head louse rarely exceeds a length of three millimeters, and the body wall is, in general, a little more deeply pigmented and somewhat tougher than that of the body louse. All stages of the life cycle are spent on the host, the eggs are attached directly to the hairs of the host. Control of this species involves direct treatment of the host and is usually considered a medical problem.

Crab Louse or Pubic Louse: Phthirus Pubis: Family Phthiridae: The crab louse is a parasite of man, and while usually concerned with the infestations of the pubic and perianal regions, it may be found in any region of body hair, all life stages are spent on the body of the host, the eggs are attached directly to the body hairs of the host. This insect does not move around much on the body of the host and may remain stationary with the mouthparts inserted into the skin for several days at a time.

The crab louse is smaller than the body louse and the head louse. Specimens are rarely more than two millimeters long. The body is broad and short and the front legs are much smaller than the second and third pairs of legs. The first apparent abdominal segment bears a total of six spiracles on its upper surface.

Control measures of this insect involves the treatment of the host.

8. RODENTS:

Rats are rodents (Rattus and related genera) that differs from mice by size and features of the teeth. Rats and mice are among the most destructive pests. They destroy food and property; they cause fires and they spread disease (typhus fever, plaque, dysentery, rat-bite fever and others).

There are several types of rats. Those most common in the United States are the Roof Rat (Rattus Rattus) and the Common Rat or Norway Rat (Rattus Norvegicus). The common rat and the house mouse (Mus Musculus) are gnawing animals. Their chisel-like teeth grow constantly in a semi-circular form. They must gnaw to keep these teeth worn down. The common rat is called the Norway Rat, Brown Rat, Barn Rat, Gray Rat and other aliases. They are very prevalent. Conservative estimates place their numbers far above the human population.

The rat is a vicious enemy of man. Therefore, proper controls are necessary. Good rat control measures can be accomplished only if all of the basic control measures are carried out in the following order:

1. Survey
2. Rat proof
3. Eliminate shelter
4. Remove food and water
5. Poison, trap or have them fumigated

FOOD SERVICE GLOSSARY

TABLE OF CONTENTS

	Page
Absorption Capability ... Antioxidant	1
Antipasti or Antipasto ... Bavarian	2
Beat ... Brown	3
Brunswick Stew ... Chili con Carne	4
Chill ... Croutons	5
Crullers ... Disinfectant	6
Disposables ... Éclair	7
Edible ... Fold	8
Fold In ... Fricassee	9
Fritters ... Goulash	10
Gourmet ... Horseshoes	11
Host ... Kebab	12
Knead ... Marinade	13
Marinate ... Mulligatawny	14
Myocide ... Pare	15
Parkerhouse Rolls ... Potable	16
Potentially Hazardous pH ... Reconstitute	17
Rehydrate ... Saponify	18
Saturation ... Skim	19
Slack Dough ... Steep	20
Sterilize ... Tartar	21
Tarts ... Truss	22
Vacuum Drying ... Zwieback	23

FOOD SERVICE GLOSSARY

A

ABSORPTION CAPABILITY
The property of flour to absorb and hold liquid.

ACIDITY
Sourness or tartness in a food product; in yeast doughs, a condition indicating excess fermentation; a factor in generating carbon dioxide for cake leavening.

AERATION
See LEAVENING.

AEROBIC BACTERIA
Those that require the presence of free oxygen as found in the air for growth.

A LA CARTE
On the menu alone, not in combination with a total meal.

A LA KING
A dish served with a cream sauce, usually containing green peppers and pimentos, and sometimes mushrooms and onions.

A LA MODE
In a fashion or the style of; for example, desserts served with ice cream or pot roast of beef cooked with vegetables.

ALBUMEN
Egg white.

AMBROSIA
A favorite southern dessert made of oranges, bananas, pineapple, and shredded coconut.

AMEBA
A simple animal-like organism that grows in water.

ANAEROBIC BACTERIA
Those that grow in oxygen-free atmosphere, deriving oxygen from solid or liquid materials and producing toxic substances.

ANTIBIOTICS
Substances produced by microorganisms and capable of inhibiting or killing other microorganisms.

ANTIOXIDANT
A chemical solution in which fruits and vegetables are dipped to prevent darkening.

ANTIPASTI or ANTIPASTO
An appetizer, or a spicy first course, consisting of relishes, cold sliced meats rolled with or without stuffings, fish, or other hors d'oeuvres eaten with a fork.

ANTISEPTIC
An agent that may or may not kill microorganisms, but does inhibit their growth. Peroxide is an example.

APPETIZER
A small portion of food or drink before or as the first course of a meal. These include a wide assortment of items ranging from cocktails, canapes, and hors d'oeuvres to plain fruit juices. The function of an appetizer is to pep up the appetite.

AU GRATIN
A thin surface crust formed by either bread or cheese, or both. Sometimes used with a cream sauce.

AU JUS
With natural juice. Roast rib au jus, for example, is beef served with unthickened gravy.

B

BACILLI
Cylindrical or rod-shaped bacteria responsible for such diseases as botulism, typhoid fever, and tuberculosis.

BACTERIA
Microscopic, one-cell microbes found in soil, water, and most material throughout nature. Some are responsible for disease and food spoilage, others are useful in industrial fermentation.

BACTERICIDE
Any substance that kills bacteria and related forms of life.

BAKE
To cook by dry heat in an oven. When applied to meats, it is called roasting.

BARBECUE
To roast or broil in a highly seasoned sauce.

BASTE
To moisten foods while cooking, especially while roasting meat. Melted fat, meat drippings, stock, water, or water and fat may be used.

BATTER
A homogeneous mixture of ingredients with liquid to make a mass that is of a soft plastic character.

BAVARIAN
A style of cooking that originated in the Bavarian section of Germany.

BEAT
   To make a mixture smooth or to introduce air by using a lifting motion with spoon or whip.

BENCH TOLERANCE
   The property of dough to ferment at a rate slow enough to prevent overfermentation while dough is being made up into units on the bench.

BLANCH
   To rinse with boiling water, drain, and rinse in cold water. Used for rice, macaroni, and other pastas to prevent sticking. For potatoes, to cook in hot, deep fat for a short time until clear but not brown.

BLAND
   Mild flavored, not stimulating to the taste.

BLEACHED FLOUR
   Flour that has been treated by a chemical to remove its natural color and make it white.

BLEEDING
   Dough that has been cut and left unsealed at the cut, thus permitting the escape of leavening gas. This term also applies to icing that bleeds.

BLEND
   To mix thoroughly two or more ingredients.

BOIL
   To cook in a liquid that bubbles actively during the time of cooking. The boiling temperature of water at sea level is 212° F.

BOTULISM
   Acute food poisoning caused by botulin (toxin) in food.

BOUILLON
   A clear soup made from beef or chicken stock or soup and gravy base.

BRAISE
   To brown meat or vegetables in a small amount of fat, then to cook slowly, covered, at simmering temperature in a small amount of liquid. The liquid may be juices rendered from meat, or added water, milk, or meat stock.

BREAD
   To coat with crumbs of bread or other food; or to dredge in seasoned flour, dip in a mixture of milk and slightly beaten eggs, and then dredge again in crumbs.

BROIL
   To cook under or over direct heat.

BROWN
   To cook, usually at medium or high heat, until the item of food darkens.

BRUNSWICK STEW
A main dish composed of a combination of poultry, meats, and vegetables.

BUTTERFLY
A method of cutting double chops (usually pork) from boneless loin strips. One side of each double chop is hinged together with a thin layer of meat.

BUTTERHORNS
Basic sweet dough cut and shaped like horns.

C

CACCIATORE
Chicken cooked "hunter" style. Browned chicken is braised in a sauce made with tomatoes, other vegetables, stock, and herbs.

CANAPE
Any of many varieties of appetizers, usually spread on bread, toast, or crackers and eaten with the fingers.

CANDY
To cook in sugar or syrup.

CARAMELIZED SUGAR
Dry sugar heated with constant stirring until melted and dark in color, used for flavoring and coloring.

CARBOHYDRATES
Sugars and starches derived chiefly from fruits and vegetable sources and containing set amounts of carbon, hydrogen, and oxygen.

CARBON DIOXIDE
A colorless, tasteless edible gas obtained during fermentation or from a combination of soda and acid.

CARRIERS
Persons who harbor and disseminate germs without having symptoms of a disease. The individual has either had the disease at one time and temporarily continues to excrete the organism, or has never manifested symptoms because of good resistance to the disease.

CHIFFONADE DRESSING
A salad dressing containing chopped hard-cooked eggs and beets.

CHIFFON CAKE
A sponge cake containing liquid shortening.

CHILI
A special pepper or its fruits. Dried, ground chili peppers are used in chili powder.

CHILI CON CARNE
Ground beef and beans seasoned with chili powder.

CHILL
   To place in a refrigerator or cool place until cold.

CHOP
   To cut into pieces with a knife or chopper.

CHOP SUEY
   A thick Chinese stew of thin slices of pork and various vegetables, such as bean sprouts, celery, and onions.

CLEAR FLOUR
   Lower grade and higher ash content flour remaining after the patent flour has been separated. (Used in rye bread.)

COAGULATE
   To thicken or form into a consistent mass.

COAT
   To cover the entire surface of food with a selected mixture.

CONDIMENTS
   Seasonings that in themselves furnish little nourishment, but which improve the flavor of food.

CONGEALING POINT
   Temperature or time at which a liquid changes to a firm or plastic condition.

COOKING LOSSES
   Loss of weight, liquid, or nutrients, and possibly a lowered palatability of a cooked food.

COOL
   To let stand, usually at room temperature, until no longer warm to touch.

CREAM
   To mix until smooth, sugar, shortening, and other ingredients; to incorporate air so that resultant mixture increases appreciably in volume and is thoroughly blended.

CREAM PUFFS
   Baked puffs of cream-puff dough, which are hollow; usually filled with cream pudding, whipped topping, or ice cream.

CREOLE
   A cooked sauce for poultry or shrimp. Usually served with rice.

CRISP
   To make somewhat firm and brittle.

CROUTONS
   Bread cut into small cubes and either fried or browned in the oven, according to the intended use. Used as a garnish, croutons are fried; as soup accompaniments, baked.

CRULLERS
Long, twisted doughnuts.

CRUMB
The soft part of bread or cake; a fragment of bread (see also BREAD).

CRUST
Hardened exterior of bread; pastry portion of pie.

CRUSTING
Formation of dry crust on the surface of doughs.

CUBE
To cut into approximately 1/4 to 1/2 inch squares.

CURDLE
To change into curd; to coagulate or thicken.

CURING
A form of processing meat, which improves its flavor and texture.

CURRY
A powder made from many spice ingredients and used as a seasoning for Indian and Oriental-type dishes, such as shrimp and chicken curry.

CUSTOM FOODS (RATION-DENSE)
Various types of labor- and space-saving foods, including canned, concentrated, dehydrated, frozen, and prefabricated items.

CUT IN (as for shortening)
To combine firm shortening and flour with pastry blender or knife.

D

DANISH PASTRY
A flaky yeast dough having butter or shortening rolled into it.

DASH
A scant 1/8 teaspoon.

DEVILED
A highly seasoned, chopped, ground, or whole mixture served hot or cold.

DICE
To cut into 1/4 inch or smaller cubes.

DISINFECTANT
A chemical agent that destroys bacteria and other harmful organisms.

DISPOSABLES
Disposable articles used for food preparation, eating, or drinking utensils, constructed wholly or in part from paper or synthetic materials and intended for one single service.

DISSOLVE
To mix a solid, dry substance with a liquid until the solid is in solution.

DIVIDER
A machine used to cut dough into a desired size or weight.

DOCKING
Punching a number of vertical impressions in a dough with a smooth round stick about the size of a pencil. Docking makes doughs expand uniformly without bursting during baking.

DOT
To place small pieces (usually butter) on the surface of food.

DOUGH
The thickened, uncooked mass of combined ingredients for bread, rolls, cookies, and pies, but usually applicable to bread.

DOUGH CONDITIONER
A chemical product added to flour to alter its properties to hold gas.

DOUGH TEMPERATURES
Temperature of dough at different stages of processing.

DRAIN
To remove liquid.

DREDGE
To sprinkle or coat with flour, sugar, or cornmeal.

DRIPPINGS
Fat and juice dripped from roasted meat.

DRY YEAST
A dehydrated form of yeast.

DU JOUR
Today's or of the day; for example, Specialite du jour — food specialty of the day.

DUSTING
Distributing a film of flour or starch on pans or work surfaces.

E

ECLAIR
A long, thin pastry made from cream puff batter, usually filled with cream pudding, whipped topping, or ice cream. The baked, filled shell is dusted with confectioner's sugar or covered with a thin layer of chocolate.

EDIBLE
Fit to eat, wholesome.

EMULSIFICATION
The process of blending together fat and water solutions of ingredients to produce a stable mixture that will not separate while standing.

ENCHILADAS
A dish consisting of tortillas, a sauce, a filling (cheese, meat, or beans) and garnished with a topping such as cheese, then rolled, stacked, or folded and baked.

ENRICHED BREAD
Bread made from enriched flour and containing federally prescribed amounts of thiamin, riboflavin, iron, and niacin.

ENTREE
An intermediary course of a meal, which in the United States is usually the "main" dish.

ENZYME
A substance, produced by living organisms, that has the power to bring about changes in organic materials.

EXTRACT
Essence of fruits or spices used for flavoring.

F

FAT ABSORPTION
Fat that is absorbed in food products as they are fried in deep fat.

FERMENTATION
The chemical changes of an organic compound caused by action of living organisms (yeast or bacteria), usually producing a leavening gas.

FILET
The English term is "fillet," designating a French method of dressing fish, poultry, or meat to exclude bones and include whole muscle strips.

FLIPPER
A can of food that bulges at one end, indicating food spoilage. If pressed, the bulge may "flip" to the opposite end. Can and contents should be discarded.

FOAM
Mass of beaten egg and sugar, as in sponge cake before the flour is added.

FOLD
To lap yeast dough over onto itself. With cake batter, to lift and lap the batter onto itself to lightly incorporate ingredients.

FOLD IN
To combine ingredients gently with an up-and-over motion by lifting one up through the other.

FOOD-CONTACT SURFACES
Those parts and areas of equipment and utensils with which food normally comes in contact. Also those surfaces with which food may come in contact and drain back into surfaces normally in contact with food.

FOOD INFECTION
A food-borne illness from ingesting foods carrying bacteria that later multiply within the body and produce disease.

FOOD INTOXICATION
Another term used synonymously with food poisoning, or the ingestion of a food containing a poisonous substance.

FOOD POISONING
A food-borne illness contracted through ingesting food that contains some poisonous substance.

FOOD VALUE
The quantity of a nutrient contained in a food substance.

FOO YOUNG
A popular dish made with scrambled eggs or omelets with cut Chinese vegetables, onions, and meat. Usually, the dish is served with a sauce.

FORMULA
A recipe giving ingredients, amounts to be used, and the method of preparing the finished product.

FRANCONIA POTATOES
Potatoes are parboiled, then oven-browned in butter.

FREEZE DRYING
Drying method where the product is first frozen and then placed within a vacuum chamber (freeze dehydration). Aided by small controlled inputs of thermal or microwave energy, the moisture in the product passes directly from the ice-crystalline state to moisture vapor that is evacuated.

FRENCH BREAD
A crusty bread, baked in a narrow strip and containing little or no shortening.

FRENCH FRY
To cook in deep fat.

FRICASSEE
To cook by braising; usually applied to fowl or veal cut into pieces.

FRITTERS
Fruit, meat, poultry, or vegetables that are dipped in batter and fried.

FRIZZLE
To cook in a small amount of fat until food is crisp and curled at the edges.

FRY
To cook in hot fat. When a small amount of fat is used, the process is known as pan-frying or sauteing; when food is partially covered, shallow frying; and when food is completely covered, deep-fat frying.

FUMIGANT
A gaseous or colloidal substance used to destroy insects or pests.

FUNGICIDE
An agent that destroys fungi.

G

GARNISH
To ornament or decorate food before serving.

GELATINIZE
To convert into a gelatinous or jelly-like form.

GERM
A pathogenic, or disease-producing bacteria. A small mass of living substance capable of developing into an organism or one of its parts.

GERMICIDE
A germ-destroying agent.

GIBLETS
The heart, gizzard, and liver of poultry cooked with water for use in preparing chicken or turkey stock or gravy.

GLAZE
A thick or thin sugar syrup or sugar mixture used to coat certain types of pastry and cakes.

GLUTEN
The elastic protein mass formed when the protein material of the wheat flour is mixed with water.

GOULASH
A Hungarian stew variously made in the United States of beef, veal, or frankfurters with onions and potatoes. The sauce has tomato paste and paprika as ingredients, served with sour cream if desired.

GOURMET
  A connoisseur, or a critical judge, of good food and drink.

GRATE
  To separate food into small pieces by rubbing it on a grater.

GREASE
  To rub lightly with butter, shortening, or oil.

GRIDDLE
  A flat surface or pan on which food is cooked by dry heat. Grease is removed as it accumulates. No liquid is added.

GRILL
  See BROIL.

GRIND
  To force food materials through a food chopper.

GUMBO
  A Creole dish resembling soup, thickened somewhat with okra, its characteristic ingredient.

H

HARD SAUCE
  A dessert sauce made of butter and confectioner's sugar, thoroughly creamed. The mixture is thinned or tempered with boiling water.

HASH
  A baked dish made of chopped or minced meat and/or vegetables mixture in brown stock.

HEARTH
  The heated baking surface of the floor of an oven.

HERMITS
  A rich short-flake cookie.

HOLLANDAISE
  A sauce made with egg yolks and butter and usually served over vegetables.

HONEY
  A sweet syrupy substance produced by bees from flower nectar.

HORS D'OEUVRES
  Light, snack-type foods eaten hot or cold at the beginning of a meal.

HORSESHOES
  Danish pastry, shaped like horseshoes.

HOST
Any living animal or plant affording food for growth to a parasite.

HOT CROSS BUNS
Sweet, spicy, fruity buns with cross-cut on top, which usually is covered with a plain frosting.

HOT AIR DRYING
Products are cut in small pieces and spread on slat or wire bottom trays. Hot air is passed over and under trays to dry products.

HUMIDITY
The percent of moisture in air related to the total moisture capacity of that air at a particular temperature. Usually expressed as relative humidity.

HUNTER STYLE
Browned meat, usually chicken, braised in various combinations of tomatoes and other vegetables, stock, oil, garlic, and herbs.

HUSH PUPPIES
Deep-fried cornbread batter seasoned with onions. Used mostly in the South, usually with fish.

I

INCUBATION PERIOD
That time between entrance of disease-producing bacteria in a person and the first appearance of symptoms.

INSECTICIDE
Any chemical substance used for the destruction of insects.

ITALIENNE
Italian style of cooking.

J

JARDINIERE
A meat dish or garnish, "garden" style, made of several kinds of vegetables.

JULIENNE
A method of cutting meat, poultry, vegetables (especially potatoes), and fruits in long, thin strips.

K

KEBAB
Various Turkish-style dishes whose principal feature is skewered meat, usually lamb.

KNEAD
To work and press dough with the palms of the hands, turning and folding the dough at rapid intervals.

KOLACHES
A bread bun made from a soft dough and topped with fruit.

L

LACTIC ACID
An organic acid sometimes known as the acid of milk because it is produced when milk sours. Bacteria cause the souring.

LARDING
To cover uncooked lean meat or fish with strips of fat, or to insert strips of fat with a skewer.

LASAGNA
An Italian baked dish with broad noodles, or lasagna noodles, which has been cooked, drained, and combined in alternate layers with Italian meat sauce and cheese of two or three types (cottage, parmesan, and mozzarella).

LEAVENING
The aeration of a product (raising or lightening by air, steam, or gas (carbon dioxide)) that occurs during mixing and baking. The agent for generating gas in a dough or batter is usually yeast or baking powder.

LUKEWARM
Moderately warm or tepid.

LYONNAISE
A seasoning with onions originating in Lyons, France. Sauteed potatoes, green beans, and other vegetables are seasoned this way.

M

MAKEUP
Manual or mechanical manipulation of dough to provide a desired size and shape.

MARBLE CAKE
A cake of two or three colored batters partially mixed.

MARBLING
The intermingling of fat with lean in meat. Meat cut across the grain will show the presence or absence of marbling and may indicate its quality and palatability.

MARINADE
A preparation containing spices, herbs, condiments, vegetables, and a liquid (usually acid) in which a food is placed for a period of time to enhance its flavor, or to increase its tenderness.

MARINATE
 To cover with dressing and allow to stand for a short length of time.

MARMALADE
 A type of jam or preserve made with sliced fruits. Crushed fruits or whole fruits are used more commonly in jam.

MEAT SUBSTITUTE
 Any food used as an entree that does not contain beef, veal, pork, or lamb. Some substitutes are protein-rich dishes such as eggs, fish, dried beans, and cheese.

MEDIA
 The plural of medium.

MEDIUM
 A material or combination of materials used for cultivation of microorganisms.

MELTING POINT
 The temperature at which a solid becomes a liquid.

MERINGUE
 A white frothy mass of beaten egg whites and sugar.

MILK FAT
 The fat in milk and milk products.

MILK LIQUID
 Fresh fluid milk or evaporated or powdered milk reconstituted to the equivalent of fresh fluid milk.

MINCE
 To cut or chop into very small pieces, using knife or chopper.

MINESTRONE
 Thickened vegetable soup containing lentils or beans.

MIXING
 To unite two or more ingredients.

MOCHA
 A flavor combination of coffee and chocolate, but predominately that of coffee.

MOLD
 Microscopic, multicellular, thread-like fungi growing on moist surfaces of organic material.

MOLDER
 Machine that shapes dough pieces for various shapes.

MULLIGATAWNY
 A soup with a chicken-stock base highly seasoned, chiefly by curry powder.

MYOCIDE
An agent that destroys molds.

N

NUTRIENT
A food substance that humans require to support life and health.

O

O'BRIEN
A style of preparing sauteed vegetables with diced green peppers and pimientos.

OLD DOUGHS
Overfermented yeast dough that produces a finished baked loaf, dark in crumb color, sour in flavor, low in volume, coarse in grain, and tough in texture.

OMELET
Eggs beaten to a froth, cooked with stirring until set, and served in a half-round form by folding one half over the other.

OVEN
A chamber used for baking, heating, or drying.

OYSTER MUSCLE
Tender, oval piece of dark poultry meat found in the recess on either side of the back.

P

PALATABLE
Agreeable to the palate or taste.

PAN BROIL
See BROIL.

PAN FRY
See FRY.

PARASITES
Organisms that live in or on a living host.

PARBOIL
To boil in water until partially cooked.

PARE
To trim and remove all superfluous matter from any article.

PARKERHOUSE ROLLS
Folded buns of fairly rich dough.

PARMESAN
A very hard, dry cheese with a sharp flavor.

PASTA (or PASTE)
Any macaroni product, including spaghetti, noodles, and the other pastas.

PATHOGENS
Disease-producing microorganisms.

PEEL
To remove skin, using a knife or peeling machine.

PEPPER POT
Any of a wide variety of styles of highly seasoned soup or stew.

PICKLE
A method of preserving food by a salt and water (or vinegar) solution.

PILAF
An oriental or Turkish dish made of rice cooked in beef or chicken stock and mildly flavored with onions.

PIQUANT
A tart, pleasantly sharp flavor. A piquant sauce or dressing contains lemon juice or vinegar.

PIT
To remove pits or seeds (as from dates or avocados).

PLASTICITY
The consistency or feel of shortening.

POACH
Method of cooking food in a hot liquid that is kept just below the boiling point.

POLONAISE
A garnish consisting of chopped egg and parsley served on cauliflower, asparagus, or other dishes. Bread crumbs are sometimes added.

PPM
Parts per million.

PORCUPINE
A preparation of ground beef and rice shaped into balls and cooked in tomato sauce.

POTABLE
Suitable for drinking.

POTENTIALLY HAZARDOUS pH
Any perishable food which consists in whole or in part of milk or milk products, eggs, meat, poultry, fish, shellfish, synthetic food, or other ingredient capable of supporting rapid and progressive growth of pathogens.

PREHEAT
To heat to the desired baking temperature before placing food in the oven.

PROOF BOX
A tightly closed box or cabinet equipped with shelves to permit the introduction of heat and steam; used for fermenting dough.

PROOFING PERIOD
The time between molding and baking during which dough rises.

PROTOZOA
Minute, one-celled animals.

PROVOLONE
A cured, hard cheese that has a smoky flavor.

PSYCHROPHILIC BACTERIA
Microorganisms that grow at temperatures near freezing.

PUREE
The pulp of a boiled food that has been rubbed through a sieve. Soup is called puree when it has been thickened with its sieved, pulpy ingredients.

Q

QUICK BREADS
Bread products baked from a lean, chemically leavened batter.

R

RABBIT OR RAREBIT
A melted-cheese dish.

RAGOUT
The French word for "stew."

RANCID
A disagreeable odor or flavor. Usually used to describe foods with high fat content, when oxidation occurs.

READY-TO-COOK POULTRY
Drawn or eviscerated poultry.

RECONSTITUTE
To restore the water taken from a food when it was dehydrated.

REHYDRATE
Combining a food with the same quantity of water that has been removed from it (see also RECONSTITUTE).

RELISH
A side dish, usually contrasting in color, shape, and texture to the meal. Usually designed to add flavor, zest, and interest to a meal.

RISSOLE
A French term meaning to obtain a crackling food by means of heat. Rissole potatoes are cooked to a golden brown crispness in fat.

ROAST
See BAKE.

ROPE
A spoiling bacterial growth in bread experienced when the dough becomes infected with bacterial spores. Poor sanitation can result in rope.

ROUNDING OR ROUNDING UP
Shaping of dough pieces into a ball to seal end and prevent bleeding and escape of gas.

ROUX
Preparation of flour and melted butter (or fat) used to thicken sauces, gravies, and soups.

ROYAL FROSTING
Decorative frosting of cooked sugar and egg whites.

S

SAFE HOLDING TEMPERATURE
A range of cold and hot temperatures considered safe for holding potentially hazardous foods, including those refrigeration temperatures 40° F, or below, or heating temperatures 140° F, or above.

SALISBURY STEAK
A ground meat dish cooked with onions and made to resemble steak in shape. Sometimes referred to as hamburg steak.

SALMONELLA INFECTION
A type of food poisoning transmitted through foods such as poultry and poultry products containing salmonella bacteria.

SANITIZE
Effective bactericidal treatment of clean surfaces of equipment and utensils by an established process that is effective in destroying microorganisms.

SAPONIFY
To convert to soap.

SATURATION
　Absorption to the limit of the capacity.

SAUERBRATEN
　A beef pot roast cooked in a sour sauce variously prepared with spices and vinegar, and sometimes served with sour cream.

SAUTE
　See FRY.

SCALD
　To heat a liquid over hot water or direct heat to a temperature just below the boiling point.

SCALE
　An instrument for weighing.

SCALING
　Apportioning batter or dough according to unit of weight.

SCALLOP
　To bake food, usually cut in pieces, with a sauce or other liquid.

SCORE
　To cut shallow slits or gashes in the surface of food with a knife.

SCORING
　Judging finished goods according to points of perfection; or to cut or slash the top surface of dough pieces.

SEASON
　To add, or sprinkle, with seasonings or condiments.

SHRED
　To cut or tear into thin strips or pieces using a knife or a shredder attachment.

SIFTING
　Passing through fine sieve for effective blending and to remove foreign or oversize particles.

SIMMER
　To cook in liquid at a temperature just below the boiling point.

SKEWER
　A sharp metal or wood pin used to hold parts of poultry meat or skin together while being roasted.

SKIM
　To remove floating matter from the surface of a liquid with a spoon, ladle, or skimmer.

SLACK DOUGH
　　This is a dough that is soft and extensible but has lost its resiliency.

SLIVER
　　To cut or split into long, thin pieces.

SMOKING
　　A treatment used on most cured meat to add color and flavor.

SMORGASBORD
　　A Scandinavian-type luncheon or supper, served buffet style. Many different dishes are served, including hot and cold hors d'oeuvres, pickled vegetables, fish, assorted cheeses, jellied salads, cold and hot fish, and meats.

SMOTHER
　　To cook in a covered container, as smothered onions.

SNAPS
　　Small cookies that run flat during baking and become crisp on cooking.

SNICKERDOODLE
　　A coffeecake with a crumb topping.

SOLIDIFYING POINT
　　Temperature at which a fluid changes to a solid.

SPORE
　　Any one of various small or minute primitive reproductive bodies, capable of maintaining and reproducing itself. These are unicellular, produced by plants, molds, and bacteria.

SPRAY DRYING
　　Used for liquids and thick materials such as soup. Hot air coming into a drier contacts the small globules of the product and causes the water to be evaporated.

SPRINGER
　　A marked bulging of a food can at one or both ends. Improper exhausting of air from the can before sealing, or bacterial or chemical growth may cause swelling and spoilage.

SPRINKLE
　　To scatter in drops or small particles, such as chopped parsley, over a finished product.

STAPHYLOCOCCI
　　A family of bacteria formed in grapelike clusters, living as parasites on the outer skin and mucous membrane.

STEAM
　　To cook in steam with or without pressure.

STEEP
　　To let stand in hot liquid below boiling temperature to extract flavor, color, or other qualities from a specific food.

STERILIZE
  To destroy microorganisms by chemical or mechanical means.

STEW
  To simmer in liquid.

STIR
  To blend or mix ingredients by using a spoon or other implement.

STREPTOCOCCI
  Single-celled, globular-shaped bacteria.

STROGANOFF
  Beef prepared with sour cream.

STRONG FLOUR
  One that is suitable for the production of bread of good volume and quality.

SUCCOTASH
  A combination of corn and lima beans.

SUGAR
  To sprinkle or mix with sugar; refers to granulated unless otherwise specified in recipe.

SUKIYAKI
  A popular Japanese dish consisting of thin slices of meat fried with onions and other vegetables, including bean sprouts, and soy sauce containing seasoning, herbs, and spices.

SWELLER
  A can of food having both ends bulging as a result of spoilage. Swellers should be discarded, except molasses, in which this condition is normal in a warm climate.

T

TABLEWARE
  A general term referring to multi use eating and drinking utensils, including knives, forks, spoons, and dishes.

TACO
  An open-face sandwich, Mexican style, made of fried tortillas shaped like a shell and filled with a hot meat-vegetable mixture.

TAMALE
  A highly seasoned steamed dish made of cornmeal with ground beef or chicken rolled in the center.

TARTAR
  A rich sauce made with salad dressing, onions, parsley, and sometimes pickle relish, olives, and cucumbers, served with fish and shellfish.

TARTS
Small pastries with heavy fruit or cream filling.

TEMPERING
Adjusting temperature of ingredients to a certain degree.

TETRAZINNI
An Italian dish with chicken, green peppers, and onions mixed in spaghetti and served with shredded cheese.

TEXTURE
The quality of the interior structure of a baked product. Usually sensed by the touch of the cut surface as well as by sight and taste.

THERMOSTAT
A device for maintaining constant temperature.

THICKEN
To transform a thin liquid into a thick one either by the gelatinization of flour starches or the coagulation of egg protein.

TOAST
To brown the surface of a food by the application of direct heat.

TORTILLA
A Mexican bread made with white corn flour and water. Special techniques are used in handling the dough to roll it thin as a pie crust. It is baked on an ungreased griddle or in the oven.

TOSS
To lightly mix one or more ingredients. Usually refers to salad ingredients.

TOXIN
A waste product, given off by an organism causing contamination of food and subsequent illness in human beings. It is the toxin of a disease-producing germ that causes the poisoning.

TRICHINOSIS
A food-borne disease transmitted through pork containing a parasite, Trichinella spirallis, or its larvae, which infects animals.

TROUGHS
Large containers, usually on wheels, used for holding large masses of raising dough.

TRUSS
To bind or fasten together the wings and legs of poultry with the aid of string or metal skewers.

V

VACUUM DRYING
Vacuum is applied to liquids and fills the liquid with bubbles, creating a puffing effect. The puffed product is then dried, leaving a solid fragile mass. This is then crushed to reduce bulk.

VERMICELLI
A pasta, slightly yellow in color, shaped like spaghetti and very thin.

VINAIGRETTE
A mixture of oil and vinegar seasoned with salt, pepper, and herbs, used in sauces and dressings.

VIRUS
A group of organisms of ultramicroscopic size that grow in living tissue and may produce disease in animals and plants. Viruses are smaller than bacteria and, hence, pass through membranes or filters.

W

WASH
A liquid brushed on the surface of an unbaked or baked product (may be water, milk, starch solution, thin syrup, or egg).

WATER ABSORPTION
Water required to produce a bread dough of desired consistency. Flours vary in ability to absorb water, depending on the age of the flour, moisture content, wheat from which it is milled, storage conditions, and milling process.

WHEY
Liquid remaining after the removal of fat, casein, and other substances from milk.

WHIP
To beat rapidly to increase volume by incorporating air.

Y

YEAST
A group of small, single-celled plants, oval in shape and several times larger than bacteria. Yeast helps to promote fermentation and is useful in producing bread, cheese, wine, and so on.

YOUNG DOUGHS
Underfermented yeast dough producing finished yeast goods that are light in color, tight in grain, and low in volume (heavy).

Z

ZWIEBACK
A toast made of bread or plain coffeecake dried in slow oven.